IN THE SHADOWS OF VIETNAM:
The Gallant Life of Fr. Philip Salois

JULIEN AYOTTE

PAUL F. CARANCI

Library of Congress Control Number: Unavailable at date of publishing.

Published in the United States by KDP Publishing

Written by: Ayotte, Julien and Caranci, Paul F.

In the Shadows of Vietnam: The Gallant Life of Fr. Philip Salois

ISBN: 9798858870234

What people are saying about Julien Ayotte's writing:

Flower of Heaven is a fast-paced global thriller that would make a great movie… Bill Reynolds, *Providence Journal*

Dangerous Bloodlines is an immediate page turner. Characters are well-developed and Julien Ayotte has written an exciting sequel to *Flower of Heaven*. Paul Bourget

A *Life Before is a smart, well-paced thriller that will give readers pause to rethink their own déjà vu expe*riences…Recommended by *US Review of Books*

Disappearance: The author has developed a strong cast of characters to include those that are smart, deadly, and believable. A solid story without the use of excessive violence, sex, and strong language…5-star review, *Readers' Favorite*

Code Name Lily: The Comet Line's and Micheline's work helping hundreds of Allied servicemen escape is truly a spectacular WWII account. Countless more people will learn of her bravery through your character, Lily…Stephen Watson, *The National WWII Museum, New Orleans*

Code Name Lily by Julien Ayotte is one of the most unique historical fiction novels I have ever read. The story is absolutely amazing, and its greatness is magnified by the fact that it actually happened. 4 out of 4 stars…*OnlineBookClub.org*

Julien Ayotte's writing is comparable to David Baldacci and Harlen Coben on the thriller scale…Jon Land, *USA Today* best-selling author

Diamond and Pearls by Julien Ayotte is a fascinating fictional tale. The characters are well-developed, and the writing style is remarkable. With plenty of twists and turns, the suspense was intense. 4 out of 4 stars…*OnlineBookClub.org*

The Treasure is a gripping tale of adventure without excessive violence and amoral actions. It gripped me from the start to eventually reveal that real treasure lies in the heart, where kindness and generosity prove more valuable than gold. I heartily recommend this uncelebrated nugget of a tale filled with treasure, high-minded intentions, and, yes, romance…Paul S. Stone, Plymouth, MA

Spitting Images: A good read. It really makes you think. All the characters are believable and this could really happen. 5 out of 5 stars…Sue W. United Kingdom

What people are saying about Paul Caranci's writing:

Wired is a must read for anyone serving in, or hoping to serve in, local government. Paul Caranci provides an example of how all good public servants should act. *Jerome R. Corsi, PhD, and #1 NY Times best-selling author.*

Scoundrels should be mandatory reading for all Americans who care about our country. *JMckenna—Amazon.com Review*

The Hanging & Redemption of John Gordon is scrupulously researched…to provide the most concise and precise history of the event possible—*Steve Ahlquist, RIFuture.org*

Monumental Providence has given us not only an artistic tour of the city, it is a tour de force. *Dr. Patrick Conley, RI Historian Laureate*

The Promise of Fatima gets 5 out of 5 stars. It is the best historical summary of Fatima and its aftermath that I have ever come across. *Mike —Amazon.com Review*

Heavenly Portrait is a detailed, well researched, eye-opening account of a historical 16th century event for which the evidence exists and can still be viewed. *Joe—Amazon.com Review*

Terror in Wichita is a book that will make you "contemplate" your own reaction if you were ever confronted by evil. *Anthony—Amazon.com Review*

I Am The Immaculate Conception is one of the best books I've read in a long time. You can't help but become more faithful after reading it! *Mark—Amazon.com Review*

Darkness at Dachau is powerful, educational, and thought provoking. While reading it my emotions ranged from anger and sadness to optimism and hope. Truly a great read! *John—Amazon.com Review*

Ear Candy is a wonderfully written and informative book; an absolute must read. *Coldwaterlaw, Amazon.com Review*

North Providence: A History & the People Who Shaped It is a very interesting read; informative, historical and wonderful background about the area, the people and the events that built North Providence! *Dana—Amazon.com Review*

"This is my commandment, that you love one another as
I have loved you. Greater love has no man than this, that a man lay
down his life for his friends."

John15:12-13
The Holy Bible
Revised Standard Version, Second Catholic Edition

This book is dedicated to Herbert Klug and Fr. Phil Salois, whose heroic
actions in Vietnam demonstrated their commitment to the greatest
love. It is further dedicated to Walter and Hélène Salois for giving Fr.
Phil to the world.

Table of Contents

Author's Preface

Julien Ayotte

A reporter on veterans' affairs wrote a story about Fr. Philip G. Salois in an April 2023 issue of the *Providence Journal*. Not that his life's adventures weren't unbelievably memorable, but he lived only fifteen minutes from my home in Rhode Island, and I had never heard of him. When I asked him by email if he would allow me to write a book on his life, he gladly agreed, citing his impatience at all the details writing it himself would entail.

While I recite my daily prayers every evening, participate in many roles at my local church, and consider myself a devout Catholic, I couldn't hold a candle to Fr. Phil and what he has accomplished for humankind in his lifetime, and he is far from being done at age seventy-four.

In researching material for his biography, I came across names of many veterans and ministers who owe their spiritual healing to him in his unrelenting commitment to eradicating Post-Traumatic Stress Disorder (PTSD) the ravages of war have caused, not just in the war in Vietnam, but those in Afghanistan and Iraq as well. As a Chaplain in the Boston VA Health System for thirty-five years before retiring in 2015 and the founder and leader of the International Conference of Vietnam Veteran Ministers for over twenty-five years, you wouldn't expect Fr. Phil to also hold the Silver Star for heroism in Vietnam, nor would you expect him to be the National Chaplain of the Vietnam Veterans of America for nearly thirty years!

I am disappointed that I had never known Fr. Phil before now, but I hope the accounts of his life in the following pages allow you to know him as well as I should have. He is well-worth knowing. Saint John Henry Newman, a British Cardinal in the 1800s who was a theologian, scholar and poet, and was canonized as a saint by Pope Francis in 2019, once said, "It is almost the definition of a gentleman to say that he is one who never inflicts pain." Fr. Phil, you are indeed a gentleman, and I am honored to call you my friend.

Author's Preface
Paul F. Caranci

Is there any worse feeling than that of being passed over and forgotten, especially at a time when you are sick or hurt? This book is about one man, a young soldier, who refused to abandon others, even at the urging of his commanding officer. Rather, he put his own life at risk to ensure that others would know that they were not forgotten, that they were not abandoned in their time of need.

That young soldier went on to become a Catholic priest. During one of many Friday interviews with him at a local restaurant during the writing of this book, I joked that we always meet on a day that I can't eat. He asked why I wasn't able to eat, and I noted that Fridays and Wednesdays are days of fasting for me. He said in response, "You are a better Catholic than I am."

Those humbling words haunted me because I knew the sentiment wasn't true. Just two days later I had a very vivid dream about the second coming. In that dream, as I looked into the sky, I saw Jesus and watched with hope as he descended from the heavens and appeared before me. I smiled broadly at the site and waited for my call, but my smile turned to acrimonious and penitent tears as he walked past me without even a glance. Why was he ignoring me as he selected those with whom he would spend eternity?

That moment of my dream was a personal epiphany. I instantly realized the gravity of my sins. Not only my sins of commission, but more importantly, my many sins of omission. It struck me that that was the reason Fr. Phil's words during the Friday interview haunted me so much. He was a man who was willing to die to ensure that others didn't feel alone and abandoned during their time of need. Jesus said there's no greater love than this, to lay down one's life for a friend. While I can only hope for that kind of courage should the situation arise, Fr. Phil proved that he was willing to make that sacrifice for the benefit of a few acquaintances. No Fr. Phil, I am not a better Catholic than you!

Acknowledgements

Any artistic work, but in particular a biography that requires extensive research, has many moving parts. Successful completion requires significant coordination between those parts. This book was no exception and the authors, who had significant help from many people, wish to acknowledge those without whom this work would never have come to fruition.

First and foremost, we are grateful to Fr. Phil Salois for spending countless hours with us, recounting his stories, and providing photographs and historical perspectives vital to the book. We also are indebted to those who provided their stories of Fr. Phil, particularly those most impacted by him and who contributed to chapters 15 and 16 with their memories and recollections of our hero protagonist. They include Kammy McCleary; Vincent Boscia; Gen. James D'Agostino; Gretchen Cowel; Kent "Skeeter" Cowel; David "Chucky" McKee; Rev. Dr. Alan Cutter; Sister Linda "Sister Sarge" McClenahan; Jan Scruggs; Tracy Klug Frecker; Most Rev. Richard Higgins; Kathleen Fennell; Robert Emmet Meagher; Rev. Jackson H. Day; John P. "Jake" Comer; Debbie McCallops; Ron Whitcomb; Dr. Terence M. Keane, PhD; Dr. Wayne Reynolds, PhD; Fr. Edward "Ted" Brown, M.S., Joan Clifford, RN; Martha Four, RN; State Representative Jon Brien; Martin Webster; Joseph F. Johns; Michael Tsikaridze; Rev. Andrew Rawding; Rev. Wally Te Ua; John Rowan; Jersey Joe Washart; and Geri McCabe.

Of course, we are thankful for our formatting specialist, Glenn Ruga, and cover designer Jennifer Givner.

Finally, we are most appreciative to the many people who reviewed the proof copy of the book, perhaps hearing more than their fair share about Fr. Phil stories along the way. They are Pauline Ayotte, David Ayotte, Barbara Ayotte, and Margie Caranci.

Introduction

The longest war in American history may also have been the most unpopular with the American people. Almost from the very beginning of the United States involvement in a conflict that was never officially declared a war by the U.S. Congress, a protest movement "that nearly tore the country apart" ensued. Worse, "from the Gulf of Tonkin incident in August 1964 to the Tet Offensive in 1968, the war perpetually escalated."[1]

All war is cruel, and despite the changing combat styles, "wars still resemble each other more than any other human activity,"[2] notes John Keegan, a preeminent military historian. Still, "every combat experience is different based on unique circumstances and the interactions of real people with those circumstances."[3]

War can bring out the best and the worst in people. It "magnifies virtue and vice alike," Keegan wrote. The stories are of "fear and courage; devotion and betrayal; compassion and cruelty; cohesion and disintegration."[4]

In addition to the horrors experienced in the jungles of Vietnam, from physical injury to psychological trauma, the returning troops from Vietnam were not greeted with a hero's welcome as were the soldiers of World Wars I and II. Rather, they were shunned by the people of the United States, left with little medical care, and in some cases, left homeless. It was, after all, an unpopular war at home. There was no sense of purpose and those who fought there did not really understand the outcome that was expected of them. "We learn from the wounded how incompetence and dishonesty in Washington had a debilitating effect on soldiers and combat units fighting halfway around the world. If fighting is disconnected from clear objectives and the 'right intention' for mak-

---

[1] World History: Vietnam War DVD, Just the Facts Learning Series, Cerebellum DVD. American Institute for Education. 2010.

[2] Glasser, Ronald J. M.D., 365 Days 50th Anniversary Edition. New York. Forward by Lieutenant General H. R. McMaster, Sanford, California. Page viii.

[3] Ibid.

[4] Ibid.

ing war, the moral character of combat teams disintegrates."[5]

Lieutenant General H.R. McMaster, former National Security Advisor to President Barack Obama, wrote of how "racial and social tensions, drug use, and loss of confidence in the officer corps" led to the eventual breakdown in discipline which, in turn, led to unethical conduct. Trust was further eroded between the "military, civilian leaders and the American people, by flawed and inconsistent strategies, destructive personnel and draft policies." All of these things combined to make the Vietnam War different than the other wars in which the United States had been involved.

In the Shadows of Vietnam is about one man who exemplified everything virtuous about the human race. It's not just a story of heroism in the jungles of a distant country that few in America cared about, it's the story of continuing courage. The courage to fight demons from the past that continually haunt the present. It's a story of one man's willingness to set aside his own dreams and ambitions to keep a promise that resulted in devoting an entire life to helping others reclaim theirs. In short, it is the story of Fr. Philip Salois.

---

[5]   Ibid. Page ix.

CHAPTER 1

The Promise

"Phil is well-known for keeping his promise to serve God, a promise that I believe most grunts make during combat. I know that I did. Phil's story is a great one!"

David *"Chucky" McKee*
1ˢᵗ Platoon

The weather in Vietnam in late February can fluctuate from the mid-fifties to as high as the mid-nineties. On the morning of February 28, 1970, PFC Philip Salois was getting ready to board a helicopter from his Fire Support Base (MACE) located about fifteen miles east of Xuan Loc, a city northeast of Saigon. He, along with members of two platoons (approximately 54 soldiers) from the 199ᵗʰ Light Infantry Brigade were headed to an area just south of a small village called Suoi Kiet, where the 133ʳᵈ North Vietnamese Army Battalion might be located. The mission of the two platoons was to find and destroy the battalion.

Twenty-one-year-old Philip Salois enjoying a quiet moment in Vietnam. (Circa 1970 photo courtesy of Fr. Phil Salois)

Phil had been drafted into the service in March 1969, just months after having lost his deferment when he dropped out of college at Cal State Fullerton. In September 1969, a mere six months after being drafted for military service, he was deployed to Vietnam. In his first months there, he saw his fair share of combat, trudging along the dikes of rice paddies, looking for an elusive enemy who chose when and where to encounter their American adversaries. So, Phil's initiation into combat had thus far been minimal, other than an occasional comrade being killed or losing a limb while tripping on a landmine.

While the fighting in the rice paddies was wide-open, the Suoi Kiet area was considered jungle warfare, not at all a soldier's friend. And in late February and early March, temperatures were rising and the two platoons could expect heavy humidity, scorching heat, and a bug-infested jungle growth. As the soldiers boarded the two helicopters that would take them to their destination, the silence among the men was deafening. Vietnam was not a place where you made a lot of friends, because you never knew from one day to the next if that 'friend' would still be alive. Although Salois knew a few people in his platoon, he, like so many others, opted to maintain relative silence on the twenty-minute flight to their target.

The helicopters reached their destination without incurring artillery flak from the North Vietnamese ground forces along the way. They unloaded the platoons[1] in a clearing at the edge of the jungle area. Although Salois' brigade normally consisted of three platoons, the third platoon had been left at MACE for this excursion. Salois was in the first platoon to lead out when they landed. His squad covered the rear, while the other three squads blazed a trail slowly through the jungle, the second platoon following closely behind.

Late that afternoon, around five o'clock, the lead platoon found what appeared to be an elaborate enemy bunker complex. Nightfall wasn't far ahead at this time of year, so the captain of the unit decided they would not mount a siege at this late hour of the day. Instead, the platoons retraced their steps, retreating to a clearing where they could camp for the night.

The Captain, Osvaldo Izquierdo, was inexperienced in jungle war-

---

[1] The American military structure in Vietnam consisted of the following:

Squad = the smallest unit of men generally consisting of about seven people.

Platoon = the next smallest unit generally containing four squads or between 27-30 people.

Company = consisting of four to five platoons or between one hundred and eight to one hundred fifty people.

(The companies in the 199th included Alpha, Bravo, Charlie, and Delta Companies) The E platoon doesn't generally go out. They carry mortars and are usually stationary.

Battalion = consisting of three to four companies.

Brigade = consisting of about four battalions.

Division = contained all the above. (NOTE: The 199th Light Infantry Brigade was its own higher authority. It had its own general and there was no division over it.)

fare and was not an infantry captain, having spent his military time in logistics. He had decided, however, that to qualify himself for further promotion, he needed combat experience. Because the previous captain of the 199th had exhausted his field time, Izquierdo seized the opportunity to become the platoons' needed replacement.

That night, the platoons were very tense. While they knew where the enemy was located, they also assumed the North Vietnamese knew where the American patrols were as well. Normally the men would share guard duty, alternating shifts every hour or so. On this night, however, nobody slept, fearing that the enemy might attack under the cover of darkness. All the men were on high alert. They knew all-too-well that the following morning, March 1, would clearly entail confrontational combat with the enemy.

In the early hours of the next morning, Captain Izquierdo ordered the two platoons to march down the same trail they had cut out the day before instead of taking the additional time needed to blaze a new trail with their machetes. Consequently, the enemy was waiting in a U-shaped ambush as the 199th approached.

The enemy bunkers opened fire on the exposed platoon, quickly scattering Salois and the others to the ground. The front element of the platoon was cut off from the rest of the group and, as the remaining men formed a defensive line to return fire, they lost contact with the group out front. Every platoon has its own radio, but the radio in Salois' platoon was destroyed by enemy fire, leaving his unit no way to contact the front unit to determine their status.

It was determined on short order that six men were separated from the rest, hunkered down in a clump of trees ahead of the others who had established a defensive line and dug in. The inexperienced captain had unwittingly marched the platoon right into the ambush with the enemy surrounding them on three sides. American soldiers were careful to shoot high for fear of hitting their own men with the gunfire. The trapped men were isolated for at least twenty minutes, and no one seemed to know what to do. Captain Izquierdo ordered his men to retreat to relative safety behind the defensive line until more help arrived. Salois, however, thought to himself, *If I were trapped out there, I would want someone to come and rescue me.*[2]

No one moved, no one spoke.

---

[2] Authors interview with Phil Salois on April 24, 2023.

"I'm going out there," Salois yelled. "Somebody's got to let these guys know we're looking out for them."[3]

Another soldier, Herb Klug, whom Salois knew, though the two were not close friends, volunteered to go along with him. "If you're going to do this crazy thing, I'll go out with you. But let's have a little plan. You see that boulder out there? Let's make a run out to that boulder and use it for cover."[4]

Others shouted back at Salois, "You're crazy, all you've got is that (M-79) grenade launcher, and Klug's only got an (M-16) rifle. You'll never make it."[5]

Salois and Klug didn't know who was trapped out there, but they were soldiers who needed help to get back, assuming any of them were even still alive. Before heading out with Klug, PFC Phil Salois took a moment to pray, making a promise to God.

"I'm going out there to get these guys, Lord, and if you get me out of this place safe and sound, without a scratch, I'll do anything you want."[6]

Moments later, both took off for the large boulder, bullets whistling by them as they low-crawled the entire one hundred fifty feet to the relative security of the large rock. As they took shelter behind it, panting and sweating profusely, they began spraying their right flank with small arms fire while Salois lobbed grenades from his M-79 Grenade Launcher as fast as he could load it. All of this was to divert attention to Klug and him, and away from the six pinned down soldiers. Enemy bullets began bouncing off the boulder as the two men crouched behind it. Their efforts provided enough of a diversion for four of the trapped men to make a run back toward the relative safety of their line. Others in the platoon also began firing at the enemy's defense positions to add to Salois' and Klug's diversion.

One of the four to make it back to safety was, ironically, Salois' only close friend in the platoon, PFC Nick Aragon from Albuquerque, New Mexico. Despite their valiant effort to return all the trapped men, there were still two unaccounted for. They were LT Terrance Lee Bowell and PFC Michael Kamrat, affectionately nicknamed "The Rat."

"Either they're too wounded to move, or they're dead," Salois rea-

---

[3] Ibid.

[4] Ibid.

[5] Ibid.

[6] Ibid.

soned. "Let's make a run back for our line right now while we can,"[7] Klug shouted. Salois agreed and they began crawling in the brush side by side, heading directly back to their defensive line. They received supportive fire from the platoon members who were shooting over their heads as the two focused on the distance to safety ahead of them. Salois reached their line first, looked beside him, then behind him, and asked,

"Where's Herb?"

One soldier shouted, "He didn't come back."[8]

Salois looked back in the field and saw Klug laying on his stomach, face down, and not moving. For a second time, he crawled into harm's way back to the spot where his companion lay and threw himself beside Klug. Salois tried to drag Klug to safety, but couldn't budge him. It was the first time Salois experienced the meaning of the term 'dead weight'. Another soldier arrived, and together, they dragged Klug back to safety. Once there, they removed his helmet, only to find that Klug had been hit with a fatal bullet that most likely deflected off a rock and penetrated his chin and travelled up through his head. He died instantly.

Salois was now running on pure adrenaline, prompting him to risk making a third trip toward the tree line where two men were still trapped. Two other men accompanied him this time. When they reached the grove of trees, they found that LT Bowell was dead and that PFC Kamrat was bleeding profusely as he covered one of his eyes with his hand. Though badly injured, he was able to make it back to safe ground with assistance as one of the men carried the Lieutenant's body back as well.

Within minutes, Medevac helicopters arrived to quickly remove the dead and wounded. Salois was in shock. His platoon had been decimated. Of the twenty-seven men who started out that morning, only seven remained unharmed. Eighteen had been wounded, and two were dead. The other platoon and the seven remaining soldiers from Salois' platoon left the area to seek shelter in a more secure place away from the action. Friendly artillery firepower soon arrived in the jungle area the 199th had just vacated, but all Salois could think about was, "Oh, my God, they're going to come and finish us off."[9]

One would have thought that the remaining platoon had seen

---

[7] Ibid.

[8] Ibid.

[9] Ibid.

enough fighting for a while, but the very next morning, headquarters delivered another twenty troops. There were still ten days remaining in the mission, which had not yet been accomplished. A new Lieutenant, by the name of James Edwards, an African American, had been sent in to replace LT Bowell. The other nineteen soldiers sent to join the 199th were inexperienced in combat, but Lt. Edwards was very qualified to handle the task of training them.

The inexperienced Captain Izquierdo was removed from the field, where he never should have been anyway. For the longest time afterward, many of the soldiers who survived this ambush hated the Captain for his poor judgment that day. Had the platoons blazed a new trail that morning, it is possible that they may have evaded the ensuing ambush. That "what if" question is one that Salois and the other men of the 199th would never be able to answer.

For their courageous action that day, Phil Salois was to be awarded the Silver Star, while Herb Klug, who died in the rescue attempt, was to be honored posthumously with the Distinguished Service Cross.

"I don't remember much of what happened after that," Phil Salois said. "I must have numbed out. I have very little recall. But I don't think I ever felt as close to another human being as I did with my buddies here in Vietnam. I've learned to rely on others for my life. And I've formed a bond that's closer than blood brothers."[10]

Life, however, had many more surprises in store for the twenty-one -year-old.

---

[10] Ibid.

CHAPTER 2

1944

"I love you too, Walter, but if you want to marry me,
you're going to have to come and get me,"
Hélène Henriette Podevin

In June 1944, Paris had recently avoided being bombed. A Swedish neutral had convinced General von Cholitz of the German army that bombing Paris would serve no purpose. The Allied army was fast approaching and the Germans would soon be forced to surrender the city to the French.

In August of that year, skirmishes broke out between the resistance fighters and German troops throughout the city. Cholitz, under orders by Hitler, was to detonate explosives carefully placed under all the monuments of Paris. Realizing the centuries of culture present in these monuments, Cholitz sent a message to the Allied Army urging them to move quickly on Paris before other German officers took action for which he could not be held responsible. General Charles DeGaulle proceeded toward Paris along with General Jacques-Philippe LeClerc, Commander of the Second French Armored Division. French troops, not Americans, were the first to enter the capital.

On August 25, as the French troops began entering Paris, more fighting broke out with the Germans resulting in serious damage to the Hotel Continental, a short distance away from the Hotel-de-Ville on Rue de Rivoli (city hall). Shortly thereafter, the Germans initiated a cease fire. A surrender had been signed and General DeGaulle was presented to the French people in a victory celebration that evening at the Hotel-de-Ville.

Walter Ernest Joseph Salois was a twenty-eight-year-old American soldier assigned in Paris in early 1944. He had been assigned to the 336th Ordnance Battalion, an ordinance company, but was used primarily as a French interpreter by the military because of his fluency in French. He was standing outside city hall as General DeGaulle spoke that night, when a young French girl caught his eye. She was beautiful in his mind and, when she glanced his way, she smiled and blushed slightly. The young girl was but sixteen-years-old.

Prior to World War II, Walter had entered the religious order of the Brothers of the Sacred Heart in Woonsocket, Rhode Island and had for a time been teaching at Mount Saint Charles Academy there. Although he served the order for eight years, he had not yet taken his final vows. When he attended a baseball game with some other brothers, Walter was caught smoking a cigarette by another brother, a clear and serious violation of the brotherhood. As a result, he was terminated immediately by the order. Distraught, and possibly also relieved at the incident, Walter joined the Army. Following basic training, he was shipped to Paris.

Hélène Henriette Podevin, the young sixteen-year-old who caught Walter's eye, had lived in Paris with her parents her entire life. The thought of living a life of freedom without the German occupancy was clearly a relief to many. Having only a fourth-grade education when Hélène was forced by her parents to go to work to aid in supporting the family, she had worked in an electric factory for nearly eight years. Her

mother, Henriette Hélène Podevin, and her father, Gaston Leopold Quainon, had never legally married, and in the eyes of the Catholic church, Hélène could not take her father's last name.

Gaston Quainon was an alcoholic and unemployed during most of the war years, one of the reasons Hélène was taken out of school to go to work. Her mother was a housekeeper, and the wages she earned were clearly insufficient to raise Hélène and her two half-brothers, Raymond and Maurice Quainon.

A beautiful young girl, Hélène Henriette Podevin, knew from the moment she met him, that Walter Salois was the man she would marry. (1945 photo courtesy of Fr. Phil Salois)

Smitten by this young beauty, Walter was determined to meet her. The second time he saw her while he was walking the streets of Paris with other American soldiers, he approached her and asked if she would join him for coffee at the Café Royale on Rue de Vanves. She cautiously accepted and, at first, their meetings were always during the day and in a public place. As time went on, however, the attraction between the two became apparent, so much so, that one of Hélène's bosses, Madame Assola, from the electric company where she worked, saw the two holding hands one day while strolling along the Champs Élysées.

Madame Assola, along with her mother, Madame Beauduret, casually mentioned to Hélène's

Though twelve years her senior, Walter Salois began dating Hélène Podevin, against her mother's wishes, in 1944, when she was just sixteen. The couple is seen here in 1945 in Langres, Haute-Marne, France (Photo courtesy of Fr. Phil Salois)

mother that they had seen her with an American soldier, much to her mother's dismay. When Hélène returned home for dinner that afternoon, her mother confronted her.

"Hélène, Madame Assola et Madame Beauduret told me that they saw you this afternoon with an American soldier. Is that true?"

"Oui, Maman, I met him several weeks ago. His name is Walter Salois, and he speaks very good French."

"Oh, mon enfant, don't get involved with Americans. They will love you while they are here, but when it is time to leave you and go back to America, they will never have anything further to do with you. I have seen it happen too often. They just want to use you."

"Walter is not like that, Maman. He is different, I can tell."[11]

Henriette could clearly see that her daughter was more than merely attracted to this American soldier. She knew that she had to stop this relationship as soon as possible before her daughter's heart was broken when he returned home to the States.

"American soldiers are all the same. He will love you, then leave you. Your father and I forbid you to see him again. And if you disobey us,

---

[11] Ibid.

we will send you to Grand'Mère Laure's in Langres, far away from Paris and this soldier."

"I like Walter, Maman, and I will continue to see him as often as I can,"[12] Hélène protested.

Within a week, true to her word, Henriette made arrangements for Hélène to move to Langres in Haute-Marne, France, some one-hundred-eighty miles east of Paris. Hélène broke the news to Walter the night before she was to leave home. He was devastated and they had a tearful goodbye. Somehow, this would not be the end of this romance.

Grand'Mère Laure Quainon, Gaston's mother, had been widowed twice before and her third husband's name was Henri Leon Belime. Hélène was welcomed in Langres and immediately sought employment locally. Since Langres was not a big city, and the devastation caused by the war did not afford many opportunities for work, Hélène knew it would be difficult to find a job.

Walter had plans of his own. Whether it was pure luck or fate, there was an opening for an interpreter in the city of Langres which had just been liberated by the Allied forces on September 13, 1944. He arrived in Langres in early October. Hélène was unaware that he was stationed nearby.

She had secured a seamstress position in a small clothing store in the downtown area. One afternoon, as she worked in the store, she glanced out the store window and noticed several American soldiers walk by. Walter was one of them. She jumped up, ran outside on this brisk but sunny day in October, and called out his name. At first, he didn't hear her, but after a second much louder yell, he turned to see who was calling him.

"Oh, my God," he screamed. "I have found you." He rushed to her side and they kissed for the first time in many months. A surge ran through both of them as they held each other tenderly in front of the store.

"When you told me your parents were sending you here, I immediately began to see how I could get here to see you again. And now that Langres has been liberated from the Germans, the Army needed some interpreters to understand the local people more."

"You did this for me? You came here for me?"

"I love you, Hélène. I want to be with you. When are your days off? We can meet here at your shop, or anywhere you want," he said.

"Tomorrow and Sunday, but on Sunday I must first go to Mass at

---

[12] Ibid.

Walter Salois and Hélène Podevin pose together for a photo taken in Langres, France in 1945. (Photo courtesy of Fr. Phil Salois)

the Catédrale Saint Mammès with my grandparents. We can meet after that. I can show you where everything is in Langres. It is a beautiful little town, and now that the Germans are no longer here, everyone is free to do what they want."[13]

They met on Saturday morning around nine o'clock, and she began to show Walter the sights as they walked together hand in hand. Walter noticed how the city was surrounded by huge walls, as it was an ancient fortified city overlooking lush greenery and open agricultural space that sprawled immediately outside the walls. She then took him along Promenade Jules Hervé where the scenery of the city and its ramparts were magnificent. She explained to Walter how Jules Rene Hervé was a French painter known for his depiction of Paris and the French countryside.

Langres, as she explained to Walter, was a military training area during World War I, so this was the second time the American military had over five-thousand men in the city at once. Their weekly sightseeing trips were always something to look forward to as their relationship turned to love. They were indeed in love, though the thought of the war ending meant Walter's redeployment back to the States pending a new assignment and certain separation of the couple.

It was only a matter of time before her grandmother's neighbors noticed Walter and Hélène together. They were spotted in a café one day. The neighbors, Madame Jobard et Madame Soubricas, told Grand'Mère Laure of their meeting.

"Laure, did you know that your granddaughter Hélène is seeing an American soldier?"

She did not, but immediately reported the incident to her mother in a telephone call.

"Henriette," she said by telephone to Hélène's mother, "Hélène is seeing an American soldier. My neighbors saw them together earlier today."

[13] Ibid

"Maman, tell her you talked to me and that she must stop seeing him or I will send her back here to Paris,"[14] Henriette said.

When Hélène returned home later that afternoon, the grandmother informed her of what her mother had said.

"I'm not going to stop seeing him. I love him."[15]

On very short order, Hélène's parents brought her back to Paris, assuming that if Walter was now in Langres, he couldn't also be in Paris. They hoped the separation would end the relationship, but Walter was not to be outsmarted, as within months he found a way to get retransferred back to Paris. Once he arrived in Paris, however, he received word that he was being shipped home and likely would be redeployed to Japan, where the fighting was still intense.

Desperate and in love, he confronted Hélène's father, Gaston, and asked if he would give him permission to marry her. The father agreed to the marriage, but Walter was sent back home to the states before the ceremony could take place.

When he arrived home in Woonsocket, he told his parents of his love for this French girl he had met and dated. He also pondered what to do. Before he had left for the war, Walter had begun a relationship with a woman named Noella ("Joan") Salvas, a professional dancer and co-owner of a dance studio with Walter's cousin, Hilda L'Esperance, on Greene Street. He loved Hélène more than he did Joan, even though Joan hoped she and Walter would marry after he returned home from the war.

On May 8, 1945, World War II in Europe came to an end, and the war in the Pacific was nearing its end as well. Consequently, Walter was not reassigned to Japan as was originally planned. He picked up the telephone, got the long-distance operator on the line, and called Hélène in Paris.

"Hélène, the war is over. I don't need to go to Japan either. I want to marry you. Come to the United States. I'll send you the airfare and we can get married."

"I love you too, Walter, but if you want to marry me, you're going to have to come and get me," she replied.

"Okay, I'm coming,"[16] he answered without hesitation.

It took some time to make preparations for him to fly to Paris. They

---

[14] Ibid.

[15] Ibid.

[16] Ibid.

exchanged many phone calls during this time. Since Hélène and her family did not have enough money for a wedding gown, Walter agreed to have one made and to bring it with him on his flight to Paris.

The two were married in Notre Dame de Lourdes on Rue Pelleport in Paris on June 22, 1946. Henriette finally realized that this American soldier was different than many others, as he did come back to marry his true love.

The newlyweds flew back to Rhode Island and settled in the city of Woonsocket. Woonsocket was just one of the many municipalities whose economy was driven by the mill industry. The first mill in the United States was developed in 1793 when a twenty-five-year-old visionary by the name of Samuel Slater transformed the state from an agricultural-based society to an industrialized state almost overnight. With technology stolen from his native England, Slater developed the nation's first mill in the village of Pawtucket in the Town of North Providence, thereby igniting an industrial revolution. Nicknamed "Slater the Traitor" by British loyalists, young Samuel ignited a spark that changed the course of history.

Soon, other wealthy Rhode Islanders opened similar style cotton mills in many other cities and towns throughout the state. In Walter's native city of Woonsocket, these mills dotted the banks of the Blackstone River, an energy source used to power the mills.

Naturally, on several occasions over the next year, there were awkward moments when Cousin Hilda visited the family, and Joan tagged along. It took some time for Hilda and Joan to realize that Hélène was here to stay.

After two years of heavenly bliss, Walter and Hélène greeted the arrival of their first-born, Philip Gaston Salois.

CHAPTER 3

Not Your Ordinary Childhood

"In a nine-month period,
Phil lost all three of his grandparents. "
The authors

Phil Salois was born on November 22, 1948 in Woonsocket, Rhode Island. His mother, Hélène, wanted to name him after one of the apostles, preferring not to name him Gaston after her own father. She said Americans would pronounce it wrong instead of using the correct French pronunciation. She also did not like the names Bartholomew, Matthew or Jude, and John was too common a name, so she settled on Philip Gaston Salois.

His father, Walter, had a strong Catholic faith, which he seemed to have passed on to his wife Hélène who was not very devout of her own accord. In fact, before she met Walter, she, like so many people in France, were Catholic in name only. Many never practiced their religion, other than going to Mass on Sunday mornings.

Following World War II, the population of Woonsocket began to grow at a rapid

Undated photograph of the Lafayette Worsted Mill in Woonsocket, RI, the mill in which Walter Salois worked for many years until it was completely destroyed by fire as a result of Hurricane Diane in August 1955. (Internet photo)

rate. The textile industry was still booming in the state, and mills were still cropping up in many cities as fast as they could be built. Walter had a background in accounting and was able to secure employment at the Lafayette Worsted Mill, while Hélène worked as a seamstress at Finkelstein's Factory on Singleton Street. Walter's mother, Eva, did not work, though his father worked at the U.S. Rubber Shop. The rubber shop was instrumental in making rubber tanks to be used as decoys during World War II. The work was strenuous, but it allowed the family to live comfortably and build a future for themselves.

In August 1948, Hélène, in her sixth month of pregnancy, received word that her father Gaston had died. She flew to Paris, without accompaniment, to bury her father. Phil was born three months later in November, and just three months after his birth Hélène realized that it would not be feasible for her widowed mother to live by herself in Paris. She convinced her husband Walter that Henriette should live with them on Angel Street in Woonsocket. So, baby Philip's grandmother became his nanny until her death on May 2, 1966. Interestingly, Henriette, in all her years living in the United States, never became a naturalized citizen and never learned to speak English.

In 1956, when Phil was eight-years-old, he suffered from a severe case of bronchial asthma. On October 6th of that same year, his father also found himself out of work when the Lafayette Worsted Mill was destroyed by fire and burnt to the ground. The owners had neither the money, nor enough insurance coverage, to rebuild the mill, and Walter lost his job. During this time, both power and labor costs had climbed significantly, attributable in part to the formation of the textile union that had organized years earlier to boost mill workers' wages. Lower labor costs in the South were more appealing, and many mills had already closed by 1956. One can only wonder if the destruction of the Lafayette Mill by fire eliminated the inevitable layoffs that were likely to follow anyway.

Phil's doctor had informed his parents that Phil's condition would greatly improve if they moved to a warmer and less humid climate which would be healthier for his asthma. So, Walter decided to leave for California to find both work and a new home. It was in those days that the axiom was heard over and over again, "Go West, Young Man," because it was the land of opportunity. It took him nearly a year to secure a job there and to find affordable and suitable housing for the family before he returned to Woonsocket to prepare for their move out West. Eventually, Walter was offered and accepted an accounting position with an established company called Challenge Cream and Butter Association, a company that had built its reputation on manufacturing and selling the highest quality butter in the West.

They loaded a U-Haul trailer onto their 1955 yellow and white Ford Fairlane and began the week-long journey to Covina, California, about twenty-two miles east of Los Angeles. The three-thousand-mile trip was very tiresome as Walter and Hélène shared the front seat of the car, while Phil sat in the back with his grandmother, Henriette. Driving through the southern states in the summer of 1957 was hot and humid and a 1955

Fairlane did not have the luxury of air conditioning. Consequently, Phil suffered with his asthma for much of the week-long trip. But they finally arrived at their new home, a beautiful three-bedroom ranch house at 19736 Groverdale Street in Covina. It was a perfect size for the family.

* * *

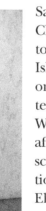

In his first few years of schooling before the family moved to California, Phil had attended Mount Saint Francis Orphanage and School on Saint Joseph Street at the foot of Mount Saint Charles Academy. He attended kindergarten to second grade there in Woonsocket, Rhode Island. The school was staffed by nuns of the order of the Franciscan Missionaries of Mary, a teaching order. Once they reached California, Walter soon realized that the family could not afford to continue to send Phil to a Catholic school in that state, due to the very high tuition costs. So, Phil was enrolled in Charter Oak Elementary from third grade through the sixth grade, followed by his junior high school years at Sunflower School, and culminated by four years at Charter Oak High School in Covina.

Top: Seventeen-year-old Phil Salois and his date, Pamela Baird, pose for the high school Valentine Ball photo in February 1965. Bottom: The following year, Phil accompanied Sandy Koizumi to his senior prom at California's Charter Oak High School.

He had never really enjoyed participating in organized sports programs through his school years, although he did play Little League Baseball for three years as a right field-

Phil attended Charter Oak High School in Covina, California from 1963 to 1966. He is pictured here in grade 10 (left), grade 11 (middle), and grade 12 (right).

er and earned the nickname "Slugger." He earned that nickname after hitting a home run. Ironically, it was the only one he ever hit in three years with his team. In high school, he belonged to the wrestling team and sang high baritone and sometimes tenor in the A Cappella Choir. He also sang in his parish choir at Saint Louise de Marillac Church. Phil never had a serious relationship with any girl in high school, but dated Linda Shugg as a sophomore, a girl he got along with fondly for a time.

One of the highlights of his high school years, when he was fifteen, was his mother's dream of taking Phil to France to visit and meet all his cousins. Because his father could only afford to send Hélène and Phil to France, Walter stayed home to work and to keep company with Hélène's mother, Henriette. Besides, his boss would have never allowed him time off from work for a whole summer. Hélène, being a 'sweat shop' worker, the name given to seamstresses because of the poor working conditions they were forced to endure at the factory, could easily find work when she and Phil returned home at the end of the summer. For Phil, this opportunity to meet all of his mother's relatives would become a lasting memory never to be forgotten.

That same summer, Walter's parents celebrated their fiftieth wedding anniversary with a big party at the Embassy Club Restaurant in Woonsocket in June 1964. Walter could not fly from California to attend the party, having spent most of his life savings on his wife's and Phil's summer trip to France.

Just over a year later in November 1965, the family learned of the sudden death of Walter's mother, Eva Salois, Phil's grandmother. Phil's father flew home to Woonsocket to help his father and his sister, Jeannette, deal with the funeral arrangements. Jeannette had never married and lived with Phil's grandparents.

Then on May 2, 1966, one month before Phil's high school graduation, his maternal grandmother, Henriette, passed away. She had earlier taken a bad fall and fractured a hip. This had led to more failing health to the point of her being placed in a nursing home facility in Glendora, California where she remained until her death.

Because she had never really practiced her Catholic faith or attended Mass on Sundays with the rest of the family, Monsignor Walsh, the pastor of the church Phil's family attended, Saint Louise de Marillac Catholic Church in Covina, hesitated in allowing her to have a Funeral Mass. The family pleaded with Fr. Walsh who subsequently relented and allowed the Funeral Mass to take place. Henriette was buried in Queen of Heaven Cemetery in Rowland Heights, California.

At the beginning of June 1966, Phil's cousin, Hilda L'Esperance and her dance studio partner, Joan Salvas (Walter's former flame), made an extensive trip to Hollywood for a professional photo shoot to promote their dance studio business in Woonsocket. They decided to take Walter's father, George Salois, and his sister Jeannette along with them. Grandfather George and Aunt Jeannette would stay with the family in Covina while Hilda and Joan tended to their business affairs in Hollywood. They all remained in California for Phil's upcoming commencement, a wonderful gift in and of itself for his graduation.

On July 2nd, just before they were scheduled to return to Rhode Island, Hélène's closest friend and co-worker, Angie Aguilera, and her husband Joe, invited the entire family to their home in Monterrey Park. She wanted to meet Walter's father and sister. George Salois was a lifetime piano player, though he had never taken a piano lesson, rather playing most tunes by ear. When he noticed a piano in Angie's home, he asked if he could play for them and they graciously approved. George started to play and suddenly stopped, keeled over, grabbed his chest, and fell to the floor. Joe Aguilera called the emergency number for an ambulance, but George had suffered a major cardiac arrest and never recovered.

Walter was now faced with making arrangements to fly back to Woonsocket, Rhode Island with his father's body and his sister. George's funeral was held in Our Lady Queen of Martyrs Church in Woonsocket, with his burial alongside his wife Eva in Saint Jean Baptiste Cemetery in Bellingham, Massachusetts, the nearest town bordering Woonsocket.

So, within a two-month time period, Phil had lost his maternal grandmother and paternal grandfather. In a nine-month period, Phil had lost all three of his grandparents. Needless to say, it was a year of extreme sorrow for the Salois family.

Following his high school graduation in 1966, Phil enrolled at Cal Fullerton State College, but ended up dropping out after only one year. His father had encouraged him to go to college, but Phil's heart just wasn't in it, and his poor grades led to his decision to drop out and find a job instead. This proved to be a mistake that would have dire consequences a little over a year later.

Phil was nineteen and unsure of what he should do next. Fortunately for him, he was able to land a job with Employers Insurance of Wausau in Los Angeles as a mailroom clerk and supply clerk. The company was headquartered in Wausau, Wisconsin, but had just opened a branch on Wilshire Boulevard in Los Angeles. The company had relocated key executives to the new branch, mostly of Polish or German descent. Those employees were very patriotic.

By the beginning of March 1969, after having been employed at the insurance company for just fifteen months, he received a draft notice from Uncle Sam instructing him to report for active duty on March 10th of that year. The notice said that he had to serve for a period of six years, two years of active duty, two years of inactive service, and two years of active reserve. The notice also stated that if some of his active duty was in a war zone, the inactive duty obligation could be waived. The deferment he had received when entering college was terminated when he had dropped out of college.

At first, he thought about fleeing the country for Canada to avoid entering the service, but realizing that his father had served in the Army in World War II and that his mother was a World War II survivor, he just couldn't do something that would bring shame to them.

At the draft board, following his physical exam with a whole bunch of other strangers standing alongside him in their skivvies, a drill sergeant lined all the men in a row and asked them to count off from one to five. This would be repeated for the thirty men in the line. Phil had counted out "Four."

"All the number "Fives," take one step forward and turn right," the drill sergeant yelled out. "You are headed for the United States Marine Corps at Camp Pendleton. The rest of you will be on buses headed to Fort Ord in Monterey, California for basic infantry training," he continued.

Fort Ord, now a national park that was designated a national monument by President Barack Obama on April 20, 2012, was a staging area

Typical barrack buildings of Fort Ord in Monterey California. Fr. Phil would have lived in barracks such as these during his several months of basic training in 1969. (Internet photo)

for units departing for Southeast Asia in 1969. The United States, at one time, housed as many as fifty thousand troops at the installation.[17] Phil could never have guessed what horror he was heading into when he was deployed to Vietnam just six months later.

---

[17] Wikipedia, The Free Encyclopedia, https://en.wikipedia.org/wiki/Fort_Ord.

CHAPTER 4

Boot Camp Luxuries

"In 1969-70, my [memory] of Phil...was that of a skinny little red-haired kid who was new to the unit, and I didn't put much stock in him. That must have been part of the reason I was so amazed at the bravery I witnessed on March 1ˢᵗ. I think of that day every day!"

Former Sergeant Kent "Skeeter" Cowel
2ⁿᵈ Platoon

The bus ride to Fort Ord took about five hours, and Phil and the other soon-to-be Army infantrymen had little to say along the way. Very few, if any, of the recruits knew each other before that day and had very little in common.

Phil was naïve. Here he was, just twenty-years-old and away from home for the first time by himself. There's a strange feeling that comes over you when you have no idea what to expect once you arrive at boot camp. He was about to learn about the unexpected, and it wasn't going to be a pretty sight.

Once they arrived at Fort Ord, they were assigned to specific barracks and given their Army clothing. They were herded off to get their haircuts, which resulted in their heads being buzzed. They all came back looking like bald eagles. Sooner than expected, they were faced with a screaming drill sergeant very skilled at the art of critically demeaning every soldier lined up in the barracks. In the eyes of the men arriving for basic training, drill sergeants appeared intimidating, insulting and downright mean. Their roles were to prepare men to be physically fit and ready for combat. It was not at all surprising that every soldier in training was called either a maggot or a cockroach by these non-commissioned officers.

Fort Ord was located right on the Pacific Ocean in northern California, and the nights tended to be cooler than Phil had been accustomed to in the Los Angeles-Covina area to the south. So, you wouldn't expect that the windows in the barracks would be kept open at night in the month of March. Because of the prominence of meningitis spreading through the barracks, a malady that was very contagious, drill sergeants insisted that all windows in the barracks be kept open at least six inches. Consequently, the soldiers would joke that while opening the windows would keep meningitis cases under control, everyone in the barracks would catch pneumonia due to frigid temperatures at night.

At the end of each day of training, most of the soldiers were exhausted. However, when the end of the day arrived on Fridays, all the soldiers went to the Enlisted Men's club to unwind and drink beer. In Fort Ord, as in most training facilities, non-commissioned officers like drill sergeants had their own social clubs. So, the two groups never mingled with each other.

Life in the barracks never allowed anyone to get lonely, as all the men tended to support each other throughout training. While Phil may have enjoyed the companionship and collaboration, living with so many men also had its downside. For Phil, sleeping in quarters with several other people was a new experience, as he had been used to always having a room to himself at home. Bathrooms in the barracks were crude at best and were called latrines for good reason. Toilets were all lined up in a row with no partitions between them. Urinals had the same arrangement. The word modesty seemed to be gone from their vocabulary.

Phil was overweight when he arrived at boot camp, and the rigors of extensive exercising, running and marches were very difficult for him. Basic training was scheduled to be six weeks long, followed by six weeks of advanced infantryman training (AIT). At the end of basic training, each soldier had to pass a physical training test before being allowed to move on to AIT. Phil failed his physical training test and was placed in special additional training for three to four more weeks, hoping the additional training would enable him to pass the test and move on.

Because of this diversion, he was no longer with the original soldiers from his basic training group as they had moved on several weeks earlier. After two months of physical training, Phil had lost over fifty pounds and his waistline had dropped to twenty-eight inches in size, the lowest it had been in years. When he completed his AIT six weeks later, he was with a totally different group of men, none of whom he had bonded with longer than six weeks. That's when he received word that he and the others from his unit were being deployed to Vietnam.

When they arrived in Vietnam, they were immediately assigned to the 90th Replacement Battalion in Long Binh for a two-week indoctrination on Vietnam warfare tactics. From there, Phil was then assigned to the 199th Light Infantry Brigade, 3rd Battalion, 7th Infantry Regiment, Alpha Company, 2nd Platoon.

Long Binh was the Army's largest base located in the former South Vietnam. It was situated between Bien Hoa, the location of a large American airbase, and Saigon, the capital of South Vietnam.

During the Vietnam War, the U.S. Army used the base as a logistics and command center. The base was a kind of island for U.S. troops "in country," a phrase used to describe a soldier who was on a tour of duty in South Vietnam. A virtual city of some 60,000 people at its height, Long Binh Post had dental clinics, large restaurants, snack bars, a photo lab, a wood shop, post offices, swimming pools, basketball and tennis courts, a golf driving range, laundromats, and even a Chase Manhattan Bank branch.[18] But these were luxuries that weren't meant for long-term enjoyment.

It didn't take very long for Phil to discover that the bathroom accommodations he had adapted to in the barracks were far better than the makeshift latrines he had to use while he was on patrol in the rice fields or in the jungles. Worse, soldiers needed to rely on their newly acquired horticultural knowledge of leaves and bushes to know which ones could be used as toilet paper without catching some nasty poison or disease along the way.

He also found out quickly that the constant walking in muddy terrain across streams and jungle landscape could cause various infections. He was taken out of the field twice during his time in Vietnam. The first time was due to a case of jungle rot, a foot immersion condition which causes your feet and toes to turn numb and either red or blue from a decrease in blood flow to that area due to the foot's constant exposure to moisture. He was relegated to bed rest and forced to treat the condition in the barracks by soaking his feet in some saline solution. This went on for nearly a month. The length of time was necessary because jungle rot is contagious, and Phil could have easily passed it on to others with the slightest contact.

On a different occasion, while trudging through the jungle behind another soldier, the branch that the preceding soldier released snapped

---

[18] Moore, Ryan, Long Binh Post and the Vietnam War. Library of Congress Blogs, August 2, 2017. https://blogs.loc.gov/maps/2017/08/long-binh/.

right back onto Phil's face. A leaf on the branch contained a nest of red ants and Phil was bitten by one very close to his eye. Nicknamed Fire Ants because of their color and nasty bite, these red insects are actually called Weaver Ants because they weave leaves together to make their nest. Men running from bullets have been known to stop if they ran into a nest of Fire Ants because the insect's bite sometimes hurt more than a bullet.[19] Phil's eye immediately turned red and became very swollen. The redness lasted for three days, while the eye swelling remained for nearly a week. He had never been in a jungle before, and the sight of huge spider webs was frightening. Spiders and scorpions were the size of small crabs, enough to inflict fear into the heart of even the bravest man or woman.

There was a large variety of poisonous snakes in the jungle, but the one most terrifying was the Bamboo Viper, nicknamed "Two-Step Viper" due to the deadly poison it transmitted through its bite. Its venom was so lethal that once bitten, a man could easily die within the time required to take only "two-steps". So, when infantrymen would see any trace of these vipers in the area in which they were setting up camp, they simply picked up and moved to a different location, rather than remain and try to kill the snake. If there was one snake there, you could be certain there were others hiding nearby.

Each day on patrol was accompanied by its own set of unique events. One day, while walking on a trail in the jungle with his unit, Phil overheard on the radio that a file of elephants had started crossing a path directly in front of them. The radioman asked what they should do? The response over the radio from the commanding officer was quite humorous as he stated simply, "let them through."[20]

---

[19] Antwiki, The Ants of Vietnam, https://search.yahoo.com/yhs/search?hspart=tro&hsimp=yhs-freshy&grd=1&action=nt&type=Y219_F163_204671_102220&p=red+ants+found+in+the+jungles+of+vietnam.

[20] Written comments submitted by Phil Salois to the authors, May 28, 2023.

CHAPTER 5

The Long Journey Home

"I went into my Vietnam closet where I stayed for many years."
Fr. Philip Salois

Following the ambush in Suoi Kiet on March 1, 1970, PFC Salois had been told he would be awarded the Distinguished Service Cross, and that his fallen comrade, Herb Klug, would receive the Medal of Honor posthumously. As it turned out later, the two awards were reduced a notch meaning that PFC Salois would receive the Silver Star, and Herb Klug, the Distinguished Service Cross. Apparently, the more prestigious medals seemed to be awarded only to higher ranking soldiers.

Nonetheless, in the months that followed, Salois was tormented by guilt, a guilt even though sometimes undetected that remained with him for decades. The rescue of the six trapped soldiers in the Vietnamese jungle of Suoi Kiet had been

Left: The Distinguished Service Cross awarded to Herbert Klug is given to a person who, while serving in the U.S. Army, has distinguished himself by exceptionally meritorious service to the government in a duty of great responsibility. The award is a government acknowledgement that what Klug did was clearly exceptional. (Internet photo)

Right: Fr. Phil Salois was awarded the Silver Star, the third highest military combat decoration. This medal is awarded to those who "demonstrate bravery and exceptional service under fire."

his idea. Maybe Herb Klug would still be alive if Salois hadn't insisted on going out to rescue the other men. The trauma would remain hidden in his mind for years. As he often stated, "I went into my Vietnam closet where I stayed for many years."[21]

In July 1970, Salois heard of an opening for a clerk typist job, a position that had recently been vacated by a soldier who was headed home after reaching his date of expected return from overseas (DEROS). Salois approached the Captain in charge with his request.

"Captain, I know how to type. I was a pencil pusher before I got into the Army. I'll take that job."

"Good, you've got it," the Captain replied.

"Just let me go on my R&R in Hong Kong first," Salois suggested.

"No," the Captain replied emphatically. "We need somebody now."

"Never mind the R&R then. I'll take the job now," Salois acknowledged.[22] He just wanted to get out of the combat fields, and the sooner the better.

There was a policy that if a soldier had six months or less to serve in the Army, he could be discharged immediately without being assigned to a fort to complete his two-year obligation. Phil had only six months and twelve days remaining to his service time, and if he extended his tour of duty in Vietnam by those twelve days, he could get discharged from the Army clean and clear and be totally released from the military.

Salois' DEROS was October 12, and the months of July through early October seemed to fly by quickly. Finally, his departure day arrived, and he hopped on a plane for home. It was a Northwest Airlines jet with real live American stewardesses on board, a refreshing sight to tired soldiers. The first leg of the journey took him to Tokyo, Japan for refueling, followed by a second refueling at Elmendorf Air Force Base in Anchorage, Alaska. From there, it was a direct flight to Travis Air Force Base in San Francisco. Everyone on board was greeted and bussed to Oakland Army Base for a steak dinner before being processed out of the Army.

Most of the returning soldiers on the plane with Salois were aware of the negative reaction the people of the United States had to the war in Vietnam, and the returning soldiers who served there. For that reason, the first step for Salois and most other veterans with him at the San Francisco Airport was the men's room to change into civilian clothes. It didn't matter. Their cropped hair and the duffle bag they carried made them easily recognizable to even the most casual observer. Salois

---

[21] Authors interview with Phil Salois on April 24, 2023.

[22] Ibid.

quietly boarded a Northwest Airlines flight to Los Angeles later that same afternoon.

He had not told anyone, not even his parents, that he was returning that day. Consequently, there was no one to greet him when his plane landed at LAX around six o'clock that evening. He was planning to take a cab home to Covina to surprise his parents. That would have been a very expensive fifty-mile cab ride from the Los Angeles Airport. Luckily, there were grateful civilians at the airport who volunteered to drive returning veterans to their home anywhere in California for only a small fee.

"Need a lift to get home, soldier?" some stranger asked. "I can take you wherever you want to go."[23]

Salois, for some unexplained reason, trusted this man. He could have been a serial killer in search of his next victim, but Salois' intuition was to trust the man's sincerity and kindness. They arrived in Covina at eight o'clock. It was dark and Salois had the driver drop him off a few blocks from his home so as not to chance spoiling the surprise. After thanking the stranger and paying him, Salois began walking briskly until he reached the front door of his home, which he found unlocked. As he opened the door, he could hear the sound of the television emanating from the living room. He dropped his duffle bag and rushed toward the living room where his father sat in an easy chair and his mother was lying on the sofa near him. He shouted,

"Hi, I'm home."

Phil's father greeted his son with a casual, 'Oh', while his mother screamed aloud and began to cry tears of joy uncontrollably. Phil, at that point, was afraid his mother would have a heart attack as she was overcome with the surprise of seeing her son for the first time in nearly two years.

"Maybe this wasn't such a good idea," Phil yelled. His father was pleased in his own way, but quite calm. Phil had always been closer to his mother. His father had always been aloof, not at all warm and cuddly like his mother, although he was a kind man.

At the end of a few weeks of rest and recuperation, Phil contacted his former employer, Employers Insurance of Wausau in Los Angeles, and informed them he was back from Vietnam and ready to go back to work. At the time, employers whose employees had been drafted for mil-

---

[23] Ibid.

itary duty to Vietnam were required to re-employ them upon their return from active duty.

The next two years were relatively uneventful for Phil as he continued to work at the insurance company. He did start dating a co-worker there who was quite attractive, and they got very close, so much so that Salois actually thought this might be the girl he would marry. She was also an only child, and with the two of them sharing that status, they tended to argue and fight a lot. It seemed the only time they were in agreement was when they were making love. Phil never talked about Vietnam to anyone. He was living in a shell, and he had no idea in what direction his life was headed until one day in 1972, when he read a newspaper article that caught his attention.

The article noted that within twenty years, there would be a great shortage of Catholic priests. He kept returning to reread this article over and over again during the weeks that followed. He had no idea why the story weighed so heavily on him, but it prompted him to begin reading the Bible again, something he had not done since he returned home from Vietnam, where he had read passages from the Bible every day of his deployment.

He started to discuss with his mother and father the possibility of entering the priesthood. His father, having served as a Brother of the Sacred Heart for eight years in the 1930s, was a man of enormous faith and thought it was a great idea, one he should pursue further. His mother, on the other hand, having only become devout since marrying Walter, thought the idea was terrible and foolish. She had always hoped Phil would marry one day and give her grandchildren to spoil. A decision had to be made.

In 1974, nearly two years after Phil first read the article on the upcoming priest shortage, he called the office of the Archbishop of Los Angeles and said he thought he might want to become a priest. The director of vocations was not convinced that the twenty-six-year-old caller had undergone the proper discernment.

"If you want to enroll in the seminary, we'll admit you if you pass a test. At least the education you'll gain won't be wasted," the director said.[24]

He entered Saint John Seminary College in Camarillo, California that fall. He was the oldest student there at the age of twenty-six, and the only Vietnam veteran.

---

[24] Ibid.

While pursuing his studies at the seminary one pleasant fall day in 1975, Phil was walking the grounds, praying the Rosary by himself and admiring the beautiful and calm vista overlooking a valley in Camarillo.

"Thank you, God," he prayed quietly, "for bringing me here. I am very happy and at peace. For the first time in my life, I really enjoy studying and learning all about my Catholic faith."

Much to his astonishment, he heard an inner voice reply to him. The voice was clear and distinct, as if coming from someone standing right beside him, and he easily recognized it as the voice of Jesus.

"Well, Phil, do you remember the promise you made to me in Vietnam four years ago, that if I brought you back home without a scratch, you would do anything I wanted?"

He had not thought about that promise since his return from Vietnam, but now, for the first time since coming home, he vividly remembered.

"Oh, yes, Lord, I do remember that promise," he whispered.

The inner voice replied to him. "This is what I want for you."[25]

---

[25] Ibid.

CHAPTER 6

The Demons Appear

"I can never truly appreciate the limitless hazards in the life of a Grunt who struggles daily just to survive the Viet Nam war."
Kathleen Fennell
Army Nurse, Republic of Vietnam

In the months that followed, Phil began to have doubts about becoming a Diocesan priest. Growing up as an only child, he longed for the companionship that a community might offer. Consequently, he leaned more toward joining a different order of priests. On top of that, the heavy smog that permeated the Los Angeles area was adversely affecting his health. Thoughts of moving back to Rhode Island where his roots were as a child kept bouncing around in his mind. He felt a strong yearning to utilize his French-speaking skill and decided to contact several religious orders that had a French ministry, namely the Dominicans in Quebec, Canada, the Eudists in Vermont and the Missionaries of Our Lady of La Salette in Attleboro, Massachusetts.

Fate has a way of intervening when you least expect it. Coincidentally, when the La Salettes received Phil's request, the former Provincial of the order in Attleboro, Fr. Roland Bedard, was visiting relatives in San Diego. The recruiter in Attleboro contacted Fr. Bedard and asked if he would consider driving to Covina to interview Phil at home. He agreed and, following a lengthy interview with Phil, Fr. Bedard called the La Salette office in Attleboro and instructed them to mail to Phil a formal invitation to join their order.

Six weeks later, Phil had packed his personal belongings in his car and was driving to New England to join the La Salettes. Upon his arrival in Attleboro, the warm and welcoming greeting from the La Salettes truly made him feel like he had returned home.

The first order of business for Phil was to consider completing his college degree. The La Salettes sent him to Providence College, where he majored in philosophy. Providence College had given Phil credit for courses taken at Cal Fullerton State College and for the two years of courses taken at the seminary in Camarillo, leaving him with only two semesters of classes to earn the desired degree.

During that time, he served as a postulant[26] for the La Salettes, followed by a year-long assignment as a novitiate[27] in Altamont, New York, the site of the former La Salette College.

In mid-1978, Walter Salois, Phil's father, suffered a massive heart attack, resulting in brain damage which required that he be kept in a semi-comatose state for ten months. During this time, Phil was quite concerned for his mother's well-being. Walter had always handled the household affairs prior to his heart attack, and Phil asked his mother if she wanted him to leave the novitiate in Altamont and return to California to live with her.

"No, Phil," she said, "you need to finish your studies and become a priest. You have been undecided for too long about your career since you came home from Vietnam. I want you to go on with your life and finish what you started. I'll manage, don't worry."[28]

Walter Salois died on St. Patrick's Day, March 17, 1979, and Phil traveled to his mother's home to help bury his father in the National Veterans Cemetery in Riverside, California. Then, on August 5, 1979, Phil pronounced his temporary vows of Chastity, Poverty and Obedience[29] in Altamont with his mother there to watch the ceremony. In September, he began his theological studies at the Jesuit run Weston School of Theology in Cambridge, Massachusetts.

---

[26] A postulant is a person taking the first step in religious life before entering the novitiate and receiving the habit. The Catholic Dictionary, https://www.catholicculture.org/culture/library/dictionary/index.cfm?id=35671.

[27] Novitiate is the period of formal probation of a person in a religious community or secular institute. It follows the postulancy and precedes the first profession of vows. The Catholic Dictionary, https://www.catholicculture.org/culture/library/dictionary/index.cfm?id=35172.

[28] Written comments provided to the authors by Fr. Phil Salois, May 24, 2023.

[29] The vows of Chastity, Poverty and Obedience are meant not only to be a sacrifice, but a full acceptance of a life dedicated to God.

The Weston School of Theology in 1967 had joined with Boston College and five other theological institutions to form the Boston Theological Institute. For the first time, Weston began matriculating students in its theology programs who were not members of the Jesuit order. But in 1974, the arrangement between Weston College and Boston College ceased, and Weston College changed its name to Weston School of Theology.

Phil's studies there would take four years to complete, resulting in a Master of Divinity degree. In most Christian denominations, this degree is the standard prerequisite for ordination to professional ministry. While he studied at Weston, Phil resided at the La Salette House of Studies on Lancaster Street in Cambridge.

During his final year at Weston in early 1983, Sister Judy Fortune, a nun with the Religious Sisters of Mercy from Burlington, Vermont, and a counselor by trade who was staying in the La Salette House of Studies at the time, sensed that Phil appeared to be much too introverted for a person about to become a priest in just a year or so. She knew that something was troubling him. So, one night she entered his room and confronted him.

"Okay, Phil, I know you're holding within yourself some deep painful secrets, and you really need to get these out before you are ordained next year. I'm not leaving this room until you're ready to talk," Sister Judy said.

On that particular night Phil was tired from the day's activities and just wanted to rest and go to bed. But, as he watched her sitting there with a determined look on her face and her arms folded, he realized the only way to get her to leave was to tell her the story about the ambush from 1970. This was the first time in nearly thirteen years that he had shared his story because Sister Judy was the first person who cared enough to want to listen to what happened to him during that part of his life.

Several hours later, they cried on each other's shoulders. For Phil, this became a heavy burden lifted from his soul. He felt so relieved that he became totally exhausted emotionally and physically after she left the room. He slept well that night.

Meanwhile, Hélène was lonely and alone in Covina, and wanted to move to Rhode Island to be near Phil. He had her promise to wait at least two years after Walter's death before making that decision for fear that she might later regret having made a rash decision. She waited as Phil requested, but two years later she still wanted to be closer to him.

So, in 1982, she sold her home in Covina, moved to a small two-bedroom ranch home in North Smithfield, Rhode Island, and found a job as a seamstress. The following year, Phil graduated from the Weston School of Theology with a Master of Divinity degree.

On February 6, 1982, the Feast of Saint Paul Miki and Companions, Phil professed his Permanent Vows of Poverty, Chastity and Obedience. Then in June 1983, he was ordained by Bishop Louis Gelineau a Transitional Deacon.[30] The ordination took place at Our Lady of Good Help Church in Mapleville, Rhode Island, where his cousin, Fr. Armand Ventre, was pastor.

Things were beginning to move much faster in his life, and it appeared, at least on the surface, that Vietnam was now in the distant past.

Following his ordination as a Deacon, he was assigned to spend his diaconal year at the Sacred Heart Church in Lebanon, New Hampshire along with Fr. Joseph Gosselin as his pastor, and Fr. Bernard Baris as his curate.

Lebanon is on the border adjacent to the state of Vermont, where White River Junction is located. Earlier in 1979, a relatively small parish in Lebanon, Sacred Heart Parish, had been entrusted to the pastoral care of the Missionaries of Our Lady of La Salette. Later in the summer of 1983, the White River Junction Veterans Center had just released a flyer and sent it to all the local churches. The flyer indicated the Veterans Center was holding a workshop entitled "Ministering to the Vietnam Veteran." Deacon Phil was among the clergy invited to participate on a panel discussion where Vietnam veterans would talk about their spiritual needs following bouts with Post-Traumatic Stress Disorder (PTSD). Fr. Gosselin suggested that Deacon Phil should attend.

"That's pretty avant-garde for them to be talking about right now," he said to the pastor, but with his combat experience, he looked forward to attending and mentoring others attending, thinking a bit arrogantly, "Maybe I can teach them a thing or two."[31]

At the meeting, the Vietnam veterans began telling their combat stories to clergymen from different denominations. The workshop lead-

---

[30] A transitional deacon is a man who's on his way to be ordained to the priesthood. As a seminarian, he typically is ordained a deacon a year prior to being ordained to the priesthood. St. Paul Seminary, https://saintpaulseminary.org/general/what-is-a-deacon-in-the-catholic-church/#:~:text=The%20simple%20answer%3A%0a%20transitional%20deacon%20is%20a,secular%20jobs%20and%20are%20allowed%20to%20be%20married.

[31] Authors interview with Fr. Phil Salois, May 26, 2023.

er, Reverend John Brock, was a former infantry soldier in Vietnam and a Universalist Unitarian minister. He was assisted in running the workshop by two other Vietnam veterans.

As the conversation began, Deacon Phil was suddenly confronted with reliving his unpleasant and traumatic experiences in Vietnam. He was stricken with butterflies in his stomach as a queasy feeling emerged, and then a cold sweat ran down his face. When they showed a newsreel of actual combat footage, Deacon Phil became visibly restless, churning in his seat almost uncontrollably. He was so uncomfortable that he nearly rose to leave, but not wanting to make a scene, forced himself to stay. Psychologically, he was in a world of his own, guarded and silent for the remainder of the session. As the meeting ended around three o'clock in the afternoon, Reverend Brock approached Deacon Phil and asked if something was wrong.

"I don't know what's come over me, John, but those video clips and listening to the testimony of the presenters has brought back some terrible memories for me."[32]

He admitted to Reverend Brock that this had been only the second time since 1970 that he had spoken about the ambush to anyone, and it began to weigh on him. When Brock asked Deacon Phil if he wanted to talk more about it, he hesitated at first. All he could think about was his upcoming ordination into the priesthood in six months, and he didn't want anything to possibly jeopardize that day. But Reverend Brock was relentless and convinced him to at least meet the following morning just to talk.

That first discussion inevitably led to nearly six months of intensive therapy with Brock, leading up to Phil's ordination as a priest. Deacon Phil's photos from Vietnam became a source of counsel during his therapy sessions. Reverend Brock would probe, like a little dagger…body bags, firefights, screaming wounded men. All of these were discussed, and some of the things Deacon Phil had repressed for almost thirteen years began to reappear. At the end of his therapy, Deacon Phil mentioned to Reverend Brock that he had already accepted his first assignment after his upcoming ordination. He would become a curate at Blessed Kateri Tekakwitha National Indian Parish on the Barona Indian Reservation in Lakeside, California, near San Diego. He mentioned that he would be driving there with his mother, and going through Washington, D.C., where the La Salettes had a house where he and his mother could stay for

---

[32] Authors interview with Fr. Phil Salois, April 24, 2023.

free. Deacon Phil's mother would then fly home from San Diego.

Reverend Brock immediately suggested to Deacon Phil that, if he was travelling through D.C., he should visit the Vietnam Veterans Memorial Wall and look up the names of Herb Klug and Lieutenant Terrance Bowell on the Wall. The visit would be very therapeutic for him, Brock emphasized. Deacon Phil told him he wasn't sure he could do that because it would be too emotional. But the Deacon promised to at least think about it.

* * *

Finally, on June 9, 1984, former PFC Phil Salois became Father Philip Gaston Salois as he was ordained a Catholic priest at his mother's parish, Our Lady Queen of Martyrs in Woonsocket, Rhode Island. Archbishop George Pearce, the retired Archbishop of Suva in the Fiji Islands, ordained him.

Little did he realize that this fourteen-year journey from Vietnam to the priesthood was just the beginning of his destined service to veterans.

The ensuing drive to Washington, D.C., en route to his first assigned parish near San Diego, was uneventful to the point of their arrival to the District's House of Formation owned by the La Salettes. Fr. Phil told his mother of his intentions to visit the Vietnam Veterans Memorial Wall to look up the names of Herb Klug and Terrance Bowell that were inscribed on the Wall.

"Why do you want to do that?" she asked. "You'll just stir up old memories again."

"I have to, Mom," he said. "You don't have to come. Just stay here at the house and I will go."

"No," she replied. "If you're going to do this crazy thing, I'll go with you."[33]

Traffic to and from the Vietnam Veterans Memorial Wall on the Fourth of July weekend was heavy. You would have thought that with so many people coming and going to the Wall, that the crowd would be quite noisy. Quite the contrary, visitors approaching the Wall did so in a reverent manner, even speaking to each other in a hushed tone. Fr. Phil and his mother made their way to the Book of Names to look up Herb's name so as to determine on which panel and line his name was listed. The name was there on panel 13-West, Line 71.

---

[33] Ibid.

On June 9, 1984, Fr. Phil placed his hand over the names of Herbert Klug and Terrance Bowell inscribed on the Vietnam Memorial Wall in Washington, D.C. Viewing their names on the wall constituted one more step in Fr. Phil's recovery from PTSD. (Photo courtesy of Fr. Phil Salois)

As he worked his way through the crowd to reach panel 13-West, Fr. Phil began to sweat, and was visibly nervous, so much so that he forgot the line on which Herb's name was listed. He turned to where his mother was standing and said, "Would you believe I forgot which line Herb was listed on. Stay here until I get back. I'll go get the number again,"[34] he told his mother. She was compliant as she understood how nerve wracking this was for her son. Minutes later, he returned with the number written in the palm of his hand.

The Wall was constructed in 1982 at the Washington Mall in D.C. to commemorate the names of the 58,196 American men and 8 women who died in Vietnam. Visitors are often so overcome with emotion that they stop in their tracks just a few feet from the panel, never to come any closer. Fr. Phil approached the Wall, counted down seventy-one lines from the top and, there at eye level in front of him, was the name Herbert Klug. To his surprise, just one line above Herb's name was the name of Lieutenant Terrance Bowell. Fr. Phil was able to trace both lines on the same sheet of paper as he rubbed across the names.

---

[34] Ibid.

"Herb, I want you to know," Fr. Phil prayed with emotion, "that I never once forgot what you did on March 1ˢᵗ, and how you and I were able to rescue our men that day. Please know that I will never forget your sacrifice, and you will always be with me in my future work with veterans. We were partners then; we will always be partners."[35]

Before he and his mother walked away, Fr. Phil prayed quietly over Terrance's name for the repose of his soul.

The following morning, they continued on their week-long drive to the Barona Indian Reservation in the San Diego Diocese in Lakeside, California. Once they reached Blessed Kateri Tekakwitha National Indian Parish, Fr. Phil was greeted by Fr. Richard Landry, the Pastor. His mother flew back to Rhode Island and Fr. Phil began his two-year stay as the Associate Pastor of the parish. He loved and appreciated the culture of the Native Americans during his tenure there.

But serving as a parish priest would not be his destiny for much longer.

CHAPTER 7

The VA and Vietnam

"You're crazy," she said, "why are you going back to Vietnam?
You're going to go crazy there."

Hélène Salois

The Diocese of San Diego had taken three small Indian reservations, all located within a thirty-minute drive of each other, and turned them into a single parish. The Barona Indian Reservation served as the home base for Fr. Phil, while the other two, Viejas Indian Reservation in Alpine, California, and the Sycuan Indian Reservation in El Cajon, California, each had their own church, serviced by both Fr. Phil and Pastor Landry.

In 1986, after two years of having made great friends in his ministry in California, Fr. Phil received an unexpected telephone call from the La Salette Provincial in Attleboro, Massachusetts, asking him to take on the position of Administrator/Treasurer of the La Salette Shrine in that town. The request was painful for Fr. Phil to hear. He had thoroughly enjoyed his stay at the reservation parish and the thought of having to leave was breaking his heart. But, as a newly ordained priest, he was not in the position to dictate his future. He had taken a vow of obedience, and hesitantly, but prayerfully, agreed to the new assignment and relocation.

During the two years that followed, Fr. Phil began to get involved, for the first time, with local veterans' groups. Two of those were the Vietnam Veterans of America in Westport, Massachusetts, and the Greater Attleboro Vietnam Veterans Association. Many of the local veterans and their wives, especially those with troubled marriages, started coming to Fr. Phil for counseling. As the word spread about his counseling capabilities, more and more veterans sought his services, taking him away from his duties as the administrator of the Shrine, a position he handled well, even though he found the satisfaction derived from it to be underwhelming. In his new ministry, he developed Spiritual Healing Programs and invited any and all veterans in the local community to attend. Through this work, Fr. Phil felt much more fulfilled.

The programs were always well-attended, which in turn caused more people to schedule appointments for counseling. The need for, and the value of, Fr. Phil's efforts did not go unnoticed by others at La Salette. One day, Father Roger Plante, the Superior, mentioned to Fr. Phil that his work with veterans and their families was commendable. Fr. Phil was elated for the support, thinking instead that he was going to be chastised for the counseling work that was interfering with his administrative tasks at the Shrine.

"Maybe you should consider doing this ministry full-time, Phil?"[36] Fr. Plant suggested.

This was precisely what Fr. Phil needed to hear. So, in his mind, the most logical place to consider working with veterans was at Veterans Administration (VA) hospitals in the area. He walked into the Post-Traumatic Stress Disorder Center at the Providence, Rhode Island, VA and introduced himself. The lead counselor at the Center immediately saw a need for spiritual healing for veterans suffering from PTSD and hired him to work there one day a week. This was a major breakthrough for Fr. Phil in the veteran community, even if it was only one day a week.

Shortly thereafter, in early 1989, he read that the Jamaica Plain (Boston) VA was looking for a part-time Catholic Chaplain, and he applied for the position. Clearly realizing that this ministry would allow him to provide spiritual counseling to veterans, he made certain that when he went for the interview, he would have his military awards pinned to his black priestly suit. When the Jamaica Plain recruiter saw that Fr. Phil was not only a priest, but a highly decorated Vietnam veteran, he was the overwhelming candidate of choice for the position.

Fr. Phil worked as the Catholic Chaplain in the Jamaica Plain VA four days a week and at the Providence VA one day a week. He managed both positions for fifteen months. It soon became evident to him, however, that two part-time positions do not equal one full-time position, especially with regard to employee and retirement benefits. This dilemma would be resolved rather quickly.

---

[36] Author's interview with Phil Salois on May 26, 2023.

In late 1989, the Jamaica Plain VA advertised for a full-time Catholic Chaplain. Fr. Phil was the favored candidate for the position because he was now well-known and well-liked for the counseling he had provided over the last fifteen months there. Sadly, accepting the position required his resignation from the similar role he held at the Providence VA.

In his new role as the full-time Chaplain, Fr. Phil made certain he always wore his combat infantryman's badge on his suit coat as it often-times became the icebreaker for many veterans who really didn't want to deal with a Chaplain. Fr. Phil was one of their own, a Vietnam war hero who was fully aware of their suffering, a suffering that he himself still endured.

When Fr. Phil had earned the Silver Star in 1970, it had taken over two years before anyone had finally contacted him to set up an award cer-emony in 1972 in Long Beach, California. Fr. Phil was so frustrated at the delay in receiving the medal that he had told them to forget about the cer-emony, and just mail the medal to him. He had not known anyone in Long Beach, and had no idea who would have attended anyway. But in 1989, when he was working at the Jamaica Plain VA, another Chaplain there, a Rabbi and a full Colonel, COL Abraham Morhaim in the Army Reserves, attempted to get Fr. Phil to return to the Army as a Reserve Chaplain.

"I'm forty years old," he said. "I don't want to go back in the Army." But, the Rabbi harped on Fr. Phil until he agreed to re-enlist in the Army Reserves.

"I want you to come down to the ARCOM (Army Commendation) at Ft. Devens, Massachusetts to finally get the Silver Star formally pinned on you. You need to hear the citation in a proper ceremony,"[37] the rabbi insisted.

At that point, Fr. Phil was ready to do this. The Rabbi, although a Colonel in the reserves, worked for Fr. Phil at the VA and attended the ceremony along with Fr. Phil's mother, Mayor Kai Shang of Attleboro, and some people from the La Salette Shrine.

* * *

During this same time period, the research department of the Jamaica Plain VA was working with the William C. Joyner Center for the Study of War and Its Social Consequences, part of the Harbor Campus of the University of Massachusetts. The two joined forces on an experiment

---

[37] Ibid.

to see whether it would be therapeutic to send veterans back to their battlefield. They had planned two trips to Vietnam, the first in January 1990, and the second one in June of that same year. Fr. Phil signed up for the June trip. When he told his mother that he was going back to Vietnam, twenty years following his service there, she was angry.

"You're crazy," she said, "why are you going back to Vietnam? You're going to go crazy there,"[38] she insisted.

Fr. Phil's former Vietnam buddies all agreed with his mother. Not a single one of his friends thought it was a good idea, but Fr. Phil needed to go. He needed to come to grips, once and for all, with the hatred he felt for the Vietnamese people; a hatred that had grown worse over all these years.

"I hate Vietnamese people. I hate Vietnamese food. I remember one incident when I was a student at the theology school in Cambridge. I was walking to school from the La Salette House. I used to walk to school because it wasn't that far. As I walked that day, I got a whiff of something that sent me right back to Vietnam. It was the smell of Nuoc Mam, a fermented fish sauce from Vietnam. It was coming from a Chinese restaurant nearby. I had walked past this restaurant hundreds of times, but it was the first time I had smelled it. It sent me right back to Vietnam," Fr. Phil explained. Experiences such as this one accentuated the need for him to return to that country. Accompanying him on the three-week trip were nearly twenty Marines, one woman, a nurse named Leslie Feldstein, and a psychiatrist from the Puerto Rico VA.

In 1990, the United States did not yet have diplomatic relations with Vietnam. Consequently, there were no flights from the U.S. to that country. Visas to enter Vietnam were issued from Bangkok, Thailand, so all U.S. flights landed there first. Securing the visas took two days and the June travel group spent that time touring the sights of Bangkok while they waited. Ironically, the temporary visas were made of paper and stapled to each passport, allowing the airport authorities to remove it from the passport before departure from Vietnam, leaving no paper trail indicating that you had ever been there.

From Bangkok, the veterans' group flew to the North Vietnamese capitol of Hanoi, located in the northern part of that country. For the three-week duration of the trip, the travelers would head south, ending in the South Vietnamese capitol of Saigon, since renamed Ho Chi Minh

[38] Ibid.

City after the war ended, and from where their return flight had been scheduled to depart. As they deboarded the plane in Hanoi, the June weather was hot and humid. But what was most noticeable was the stench in the air. Fr. Phil remembered the same stench when he had first landed in Vietnam twenty years earlier. It was the smell of death, rancid and putrid, and they were greeted by pit-helmeted soldiers carrying AK-47s, another throwback memory of the war twenty years earlier.

Did I make a mistake coming here? He thought. *I'm with the guys. They'll take care of me.*

The group walked to the terminal, a space more resembling a warehouse than an airport terminal. It reeked, and the non-airconditioned space was hot beyond belief. Fr. Phil started shaking. He didn't know what was happening to him, but the shivering was beyond his control. Out of nowhere, Leslie Feldstein, the nurse veteran who had accompanied him on the trip, noticed his reaction and rushed to his aid.

"Here, take this," she shouted.

"What is it?" Fr. Phil questioned.

"It's half of a Valium," she replied.

"Why didn't you give me a whole pill?" he demanded as if he had just been short-changed.

"No, half is enough," she insisted.

"Okay, you're the nurse."[39] He acknowledged.

Shortly after swallowing the Valium, Fr. Phil became calm again. Leslie obviously had known what she was doing, although she wasn't on the trip to serve as a nurse, but rather as a fellow veteran. Regardless, Fr. Phil was thankful that she had come equipped.

Once they retrieved their luggage and checked into their hotel, they met at a nearby restaurant. It was a dining experience Fr. Phil preferred to forget. Being of French descent, he was familiar with restaurants serving snails, or as the French would call them, escargot. But in Vietnam, the snails looked inedible, as if they had just been swept right off the sidewalk. Truly not very appetizing. When Fr. Phil saw the rest of the meal, he began to have another anxiety attack right there in his seat at the restaurant. The psychiatrist immediately noticed Fr. Phil's uneasiness and approached him.

"Fr. Phil, c'mon, let's step out on the balcony for a minute," he said in a calm and soothing voice.

---

[39] Ibid.

Once on the balcony and away from the rest of the group, the psychiatrist spoke again.

"What's going on, Father?"

"I don't know. I think I made a big mistake coming here. Everybody I talked to before the trip told me not to go. I don't want to ruin this trip for anybody else. I think I should go back home on the next plane tomorrow. I think I made a big mistake," Fr. Phil answered.

"No, no, no. Relax. What you're going through right now is exactly what is supposed to be happening to you. You're just the first one it's happening to. Just relax, take it all in. Breathe. Take some deep breaths,"[40] he said to Fr. Phil.

All Fr. Phil kept thinking about at that moment was, *they were right not to want me to come. I was wrong!* But he managed to make it through the rest of the dinner without a further episode. Before the diners left the restaurant to return to their hotel, they were advised that a group of former North Vietnamese Army soldiers would be taking them on a tour of Hanoi the following day. *"Oh boy, that's going to be something,"* he pondered, *"meeting with our former enemy."*[41]

The following morning, the group stood outside of the hotel waiting for their tour guides to arrive. Suddenly, as if on cue, children of all ages appeared, running toward the veterans with a look of wonder on their faces. White-skinned Americans were a sight to behold for children who had never before seen people with fair skin. Fr. Phil began to get nervous. He didn't particularly enjoy the company of children to begin with, and to be surrounded by so many curious onlookers made him even more uncomfortable.

"Oh, my God, what the heck are they doing? They're flocking all around us,"[42] he shouted to the others.

He tried to stay calm. Suddenly, as if by divine intervention, he realized that he had no reason to hate these children. They were not even born until after the war ended. They had no idea what war was, and they were most certainly not responsible for his pain. A calm did come over him, and he looked at the children in a different light, suddenly becoming more comfortable in their presence. Through this new realization about the children, Fr. Phil also began to feel more comfortable

---

[40] Ibid.

[41] Ibid.

[42] Ibid.

looking into the eyes of Vietnamese men. And, the feelings in those men appeared to be mutual, as the respect of people on both sides seemed to grow.

Later, Fr. Phil recollected a passage from the Gospel, where Jesus had said, "Let the little children come to me, and do not hinder them, for the kingdom of heaven belongs to such as these."[43]

As the veterans group toured Hanoi, they visited the tomb of Ho Chi Minh, the former North Vietnamese leader who was revered by the people of that country as a very good leader. This was followed by a visit to the infamous Hoa Lò prison, a former prisoner of war camp which the Americans ironically dubbed the "Hanoi Hilton. Built in the late 19th century, Hoa Lò originally held up to six hundred Vietnamese prisoners. By 1954, when the French were ousted from the area, more than two thousand men were housed within its walls, all living in squalid conditions.

By the time the Americans sent combat forces into Vietnam in 1965, the Hoa Lò Prison had been reclaimed by the Vietnamese. They were finally free to put their enemies behind its bars, and American soldiers became their prime targets.

Here, hundreds of American soldiers were captured and kept prisoner... Despite the given nickname, Hoa Lò was no luxury hotel. On the contrary, this is where "the prisoners of war were kept in isolation for years on end, chained to rat-infested floors, and hung from rusty metal hooks. At the end of the war, these soldiers were finally freed from their own personal hell, many of them — including the late Arizona Senator John McCain — went on to become prominent politicians and public figures. But others were not so lucky. As many as one hundred fourteen American POWs died in captivity during the Vietnam War, many within the unforgiving walls of the Hanoi Hilton...

* In addition to extended solitary confinement, prisoners were regularly strapped down with iron stocks leftover from the French colonial era. Made for smaller wrists and ankles, these locks were so tight that they cut into the men's skin, turning their hands black.

* Locked and with nowhere to move — or even to go to the bathroom — vermin became their only company. Attracted by the smells and screams, rats and cockroaches scurried over their weak bodies. Prisoners were forced to sit in their own excrement.

---

[43] The Bible, New International Version, Matthew 19:14. https://www.biblehub.com/matthew/19-14.htm.

* They were also viciously beaten and forced to stand on stools for days on end. 'I thought perhaps I was going to die,' said John McCain in a 1999 interview on his time at the Hanoi Hilton. He was kept there for five and a half years."[44]

As one might imagine, "none of the visitors were allowed on the inside of the P.O.W. camp."[45]

The following day, the group boarded a bus headed south to the Demilitarized Zone (DMZ). This three-mile strip of land on either side of the Ben Hai River "was a zone in Quang Tri province and at the 17th parallel that was established as a dividing line between North and South Vietnam from July 22, 1954, to July 2, 1976, when Vietnam was officially divided into the two military gathering areas. This area (the DMZ) was intended to be sustained in the short term after the First Indochina War. During the Vietnam War, it became important as the battleground demarcation between communist North Vietnam and anti-communist South Vietnam. The zone *de jure* ceased to exist with the reunification of Vietnam in 1976."[46]

On the way to the DMZ, the veterans stopped in Vinh, the biggest city and economic and cultural center of north-central Vietnam, about one hundred miles south of Hanoi. They also made a stop at the tomb of Ho Chi Minh's mother on Dong Tranh Mountain. The tomb, which resembles a huge lotus flower, is covered by a roof that looks like a loom weaving a silk band.

The DMZ was particularly interesting to see again by the Marines on the trip, as this was the area where they fought many battles with their South Vietnamese I Corps. Fr. Phil remembered that it was at the time only accessible by boat, but on this trip, the group was able to traverse the river via a new foot bridge "that was constructed following the signing of the Paris Peace Accord, the document officially calling an end to the war in Vietnam."[47]

During several nights in the DMZ area, the group of veterans held therapy sessions to see how the members were faring. These sessions

[44] McKennett, Hannah, Inside The Hanoi Hilton, North Vietnam's Torture Chamber For American POWs. Published on October 30, 2021, updated November 18, 2021. https://allthatsinteresting.com/hanoi-hilton.

[45] Authors interview with Phil Salois on May 26, 2023.

[46] Wikipedia, Vietnamese Demilitarized Zone. https://en.wikipedia.org/wiki/Vietnamese_Demilitarized_Zone.

[47] Wikipedia, Bến Hải River. https://en.wikipedia.org/wiki/B%E1%BA%BFn_H%E1%BA%A3i_River.

were not as helpful to Fr. Phil as much as they were to many Marines who fought here. He was, however, gratified to see the positive effect it had on the Marines.

Successive nights were spent in Hue, My Lai and China Beach (Đà Nang) where American soldiers went for R&R. Hue was the national capital of Vietnam until 1945, and where many of the emperors resided in the Imperial City palaces. My Lai was the site of a massacre attributed to LT. William Calley and members of the 23rd Infantry (Americal) Division and a war crime by the American soldiers involving the mass murder of civilians. While the veterans were being escorted on a tour there, their female guide explained to the group that she survived the massacre as a young child by hiding under the body of her dead grandmother.

"How can you stand there and talk to us when we represent the people who murdered your grandmother?" Fr. Phil asked. "Yet you still talk to us with care and compassion."

"We can't live in hate. Our country has been at war almost forever, and we must move on the best we can,"[48] she replied.

Fr. Phil could feel a transformation taking place within him as his own hatred of the Vietnamese people began to fade away.

[48] Authors interview with Phil Salois on May 26, 2023.

CHAPTER 8

MACE, Xuan Loc, and a Vietnamese Family

"For ten years I have been trying to emigrate to the United States. Would you write to the Orderly Departure Program and ask them for help?"

plea by Vietnam Refugee Family sponsored by Fr. Phil

Finally, after many days, the group arrived at Fire Support Base MACE, Fr. Phil's safe-haven during the war. MACE was located at the base of Nui Chua Chan Mountain, also known as Signal Mountain because of the radio tower located at its summit. It was here that Fr. Phil wanted to bury the silver bracelet that he wore in honor of Herb Klug. Unfortunately, a recent typhoon had flooded the road leading to the mountain, and his efforts to honor Klug's memory with this symbolic gesture were thwarted.

From there, the group moved further south through Xuan Loc, getting closer and closer to Saigon, their last destination stop before flying back home. Prior to reaching their final destination in Saigon, the group stopped to visit the Cu Chi tunnels just north of the city. The tunnels were used by the Viet Cong soldiers as hiding spots during combat. They were also used as communication and supply routes, hospitals, food and weapons caches, and as living quarters for numerous North Vietnamese fighters. The tunnel systems were of great importance to the Viet Cong in their resistance to the American military presence. As the Vietnamese people were mostly small in stature, the tunnels were quite narrow, making it difficult for any American soldiers who occasionally discovered them to maneuver.

Their bus arrived in Saigon early during the day, allowing the group to take a tour of the city. When they reached the center of Saigon, Fr. Phil was impressed when he spotted a huge cathedral with twin spires. The inside of the church was beautiful and decorated ornately. The church had been built in the 1800s by French colonists and in 1962, Pope John XXIII anointed the cathedral and renamed it Saigon Notre-Dame Cathedral Basilica.

Fr. Phil and several other veterans returned the following morning to attend Mass in the midst of hundreds of Vietnam worshippers. After Mass, he introduced himself to the pastor and asked if it would be possible for him to celebrate Mass one day while they were still in Saigon. The pastor offered Fr. Phil the opportunity to concelebrate the Mass the following morning. The pastor, however, only spoke Vietnamese and French.

"Why are you allowing me to concelebrate Mass here? When I asked in Hanoi at the Cathedral of Saint Joseph, the priest there said 'No'", Fr. Phil asked in his best French.

– The Pastor of Notre Dame Basilica posed with Fr. Phil following the Mass, which the two concelebrated. This was another step in Fr. Phil's healing journey. (Photo courtesy of Fr. Phil Salois)

"Well, because that is Hanoi and the government does not allow foreign priests to do anything. Here, we are far away from Hanoi, and we'll do it here,"[49] the pastor answered.

The pastor allowed Fr. Phil to deliver the homily, suggesting he do so in French. He said he would translate his words to the people in Vietnamese. Whether the translation of his homily was accurate, Fr. Phil would never know. But he confidently spoke nonetheless.

---

[49] Ibid.

"I'm a priest," he began, "I've been ordained. Twenty years ago, I was a soldier here in the Army serving in the war, shooting at people who looked very much like you, and receiving fire from people who looked very much like you. We were killing people that looked like you and they were killing people who looked like me. I came here to be healed, to ask forgiveness and to forgive."[50]

At the end of the Mass, when the music was playing and the choir was singing, Fr. Phil thought to himself, *Oh my God, I can't believe that twenty years ago I was here killing people, and here I am saying Mass. This is what God wanted from me, not to bury Herb's bracelet near MACE, which would have been meaningless, but for me to come here to be in communion with the people.* He could feel the exhilaration in his body at that very moment, while he was in that church.

After Fr. Phil had concelebrated Mass at Notre Dame Cathedral in Saigon, the pastor asked him if he would like to visit Saint Joseph Seminary in the heart of that city. Fr. Phil enthusiastically agreed to go. He straddled on the back of the pastor's motorcycle as the pastor weaved his way through the city's traffic to their destination. They arrived at the seminary just in time for lunch, and the seminarians greeted Fr. Phil warmly.

During lunch, many of the seminarians pleaded with Fr. Phil to send them theological books to replace the outdated ones they were still using. He also found out that, in Vietnam, attaining ordination to the priesthood was subject to the approval of the communist government. While most seminarians were required to have four years of traditional graduate studies, the waiting period to be ordained in Vietnam was much longer. One seminarian he met had been in the seminary for twenty-five years without ever procuring the government's permission or diocesan approval for ordination to the priesthood. Before he left the seminary for the return trip to his hotel, Fr. Phil promised to send some of the books that his hosts requested. Whether they would ever be received, he didn't know. Since all incoming packages entering Vietnam were inspected by the communist government, the chance of religious books reaching their final destination was doubtful at best.

The tour had reached its final night, and the veterans were headed for home the following day. Fr. Phil returned to the hotel and started to pack his belongings when he received a phone call from the clerk at the front desk.

---

[50] Ibid.

"There's a Vietnamese man here in the lobby who would like to speak to you," the clerk announced.

"I don't know any Vietnamese man," he answered, "but I'll be right down."[51]

As Fr. Phil walked into the lobby of the hotel, a man walked directly up to him and began to speak to him in perfect French. He said that he had been a French professor in Saigon before the fall of the city to the North Vietnamese who took away all of his teaching credentials. One of his daughters accompanied him as he faced Fr. Phil.

"I was at Mass in the cathedral this morning when you spoke. I was wondering if you could help me?" the man asked.

"What can I do to help you? I'm leaving for home tomorrow," Fr. Phil answered.

"For ten years, I have been trying to emigrate to the United States. I was a professional, a professor. I had everything in the world until the North Vietnamese took everything away from me. Now, I'm a street vendor, and I am struggling to survive and feed my family. I adopted two Amerasian children to a family that included my wife and our two children."[52]

Amerasians are children born of American soldiers in Vietnam. If a Vietnam family adopted an Amerasian, the family would be allowed to emigrate to the United States with the children so that they could learn the American way of life.

The man introduced himself as a Vietnamese refugee. He had with him passports of all the members of his family, photos, and copies of all sorts of paperwork he had filed. Fr. Phil felt compassion for the man's plight and promised to look into the matter when he got back to the United States.

"Would you write to the Orderly Departure Program (ODP) in Bangkok after returning home and ask them for help?"[53] he asked.

Fr. Phil said he would see what he could do. A few weeks after returning home, he remembered the request and wrote a letter to the ODP.

"This is the file on a Vietnamese family. The family includes a husband, a wife, two Amerasian children and two other children. They are looking for help in coming to live in the United States. What can I do to help them?"[54]

---

[51] Ibid.

[52] Ibid.

[53] Ibid.

[54] Ibid.

The family sponsored by Fr. Phil for admission into the United States. He was first introduced to them on his return to Vietnam in 1990 and remains friends with them today. (Photo courtesy of Fr. Phil Salois)

Within a month, Fr. Phil received a response from the OCD that the family was now considered a priority in the program, and asked if Fr. Phil was prepared to sponsor the family. He contacted the agency and inquired exactly what that meant.

"I can't pay any of their living expenses, if that's what sponsoring them means," he told them.

"No, no," the ODP agent replied. "You don't have to give them any money. All you need to do is help them find a place to live and assist them with the nearest Social Security and Immigration Office."

"Well, okay, I can do that,"[55] he replied.

While the decision to allow the family to come to the U.S. was made rather quickly, their actual emigration took another six months. The family needed to get educated in American culture at a reeducation camp in the Philippines, and to learn how to speak English. Fr. Phil credited his secretary, Debbi McCallops of the National Conference of Vietnam Veteran Ministers for preparing for their arrival in Boston months later. His Army buddies again thought Fr. Phil was crazy in doing all of this for a family he knew little about.

With donations of clothing, food, and furniture from various sources, and procurement of the funds needed for an apartment in Attleboro, Massachusetts, the stage was set for their arrival at Logan Airport in early

---

[55] Ibid.

1991. As the family got off the plane, the welcoming party that Fr. Phil had put together presented them with a bouquet of roses.

The husband and his wife, their two native-born children, and their adopted Amerasian children were all excited and prepared to begin a new life in the States. While both the mother and father's advanced ages made it somewhat difficult for them to secure employment, the three teen-aged daughters and their only son found work easily and were able to support the family.

CHAPTER 9

Conference of Ministers and Herb Klug

"I will always give credit to Phil for saving my life emotionally."
Rev. Jackson H. Day
Retired Clergy, Baltimore-Washington Conference
United Methodist Church

It is ironic that those trained to help others deal with traumatic stress are also people who themselves once suffered from PTSD. This burden is exacerbated when such experts hear of a former soldier's stress in a counseling session because much of what the patient said remains in the mind of the counselor. Consequently, the analyst fights not only his own demons but those audibly released in counseling as well. In fact, many of these therapists are former soldiers- turned-ministers following their return from war.

In the beginning of Lent in 1989, La Salette Brother David Carignan, the operator of the La Salette Gift Shop in Attleboro, Massachusetts, showed Fr. Phil a book that might be of interest to him, considering that Fr. Phil was a Vietnam veteran. The book was entitled *Out of the Night-The Spiritual Journey of Vietnam Vets* by William P. Mahedy. During his devotion, Fr. Phil read the book in its entirety as it described precisely the painful and guilt-filled memories of March 1, 1970. Mahedy was an Augustinian Friar and a Chaplain in Vietnam who witnessed all that soldiers and marines went through to survive the War. This was the first book ever written about Post-Traumatic **Spiritual** Disorder.

All Fr. Phil kept thinking about was *how many other people like me are out there suffering in a similar fashion?* After searching for and finding the author's phone number, Fr. Phil decided to call Mahedy and introduce himself. He thanked Mahedy for writing his book. In the ensuing conversation, Fr. Phil learned that Mahedy had left the Catholic priesthood after the war to become an Episcopal Priest. He also married a former Catholic nun.

Fr. Phil related to Mahedy how he thought that others like himself, former war veterans, decided to become ordained ministers and were still suffering internally from their experiences in the war.

"If we could find these men and invite them to come together at a conference to tell their stories, precious healing could take place," Fr. Phil stated.

"That's a great idea, Phil, and I think you should do that," Mahedy answered.

This was only partially the response Fr. Phil wanted to hear. He had hoped Mahedy would take some of the initiative, and not leave that burden solely to him. So, in the following few days after the conversation, Fr. Phil pondered how he might contact these ministers. He decided to send letters to all Archdioceses, Dioceses and major religious denominations asking them to forward his letter to any and all ordained priests and ministers who were Vietnam veterans, whether they had been Chaplains or regular enlisted men. Fr. Phil thought that this was a shot in the dark, but he had nothing to lose by mailing out the letter.

Within a month, he began to receive returns from ministers who had fought in Vietnam prior to their ordination. Fr. Phil had indicated in his letter that the first meeting of the newly formed National Conference of Vietnam Ministers would be held at the Marian Retreat Center in Washington, D.C. in November 1990.

A short while later, while he was at work, he received a phone call from Jan Scruggs, the founder and creator of the Vietnam Veterans Memorial Wall in the Nation's Capital. One of the respondents to Fr. Phil's letter was Reverend Jackson Day of Maryland, who was an Army Chaplain in Vietnam and a friend of Jan Scruggs's wife. When Reverend Day mentioned to Mrs. Scruggs Fr. Phil's idea for Vietnam Ministers to gather in D.C. for a conference, she shared the information with her husband.

"I think your idea to have a conference with ministers who were in Vietnam is a great idea!" Scruggs told Fr. Phil. "If you want to come to D.C. for Veterans Day, November 11th, I will give you five minutes at the Wall to advertise the conference to all the attendees, and I guarantee people will come up to you afterward and give you the names of ministers they know who fought in Vietnam."

Fr. Phil took Scruggs up on his invitation to speak at the Wall on Veterans Day. He emphasized to the audience that a conference would be held for any and all Vietnam Veteran ministers in November 1990 for any of them caring to attend. Just as Jan Scruggs had predicted, several people handed Fr. Phil the names of ministers they knew who had fought in Vietnam.

Upon his return home following the Veterans Day events in D.C., Fr. Phil contacted the ministers he had been told about, and before long, he had commitments from nearly twenty-five ministers to attend the retreat. Little did he realize that this would be the first of over twenty-five yearly conferences. But this, the first one, was clearly the most powerful.

At the conference, one minister described how he was so distraught about his part in the war that he was on the verge of suicide. Another spoke about being in the Phoenix program founded by the CIA to secretly infiltrate the Viet Cong to enable the assassination, torture and capture of as many as possible. As a result of the onslaught of personal accounts, it took three full days to allow everyone to tell their stories. There were many tears shed during those three days, but there was such a release in the end that it felt like a fifty-pound weight had been lifted from the shoulders of all of the attendees. The bond these ministers formed at the conference was truly a gift from God.

Fr. Phil thought that a therapeutic group consisting of such ministers could both fill a void and provide much needed support to all the counselors involved. One of the main outcomes of the Conference was a decision to begin to offer weekend retreats for war veterans, their spouses and significant others, designed to enhance their spiritual healing.

"You have to have the patience of a saint, and there are still a lot of missing pieces. Healing is a continuous process," Fr. Phil said. "It will never be a perfect picture, and it's not that pretty. But we can't get rid of all the scars in our lives," he added. "They remind us of where we've been."[56]

One of the ministers who attended the first Conference was Rev. Dr. Jackson Day, an ordained pastor of the United Methodist Church. He brought to the group his great talent for analysis, a deep interest in connecting the Scriptures with the experience of trauma, and a sense of organization and detail that most of the ministers lacked. Rev. Jackson

---

[56] O'Brien, Nancy Frazier, Vietnam Memorial Veterans Find Healing, La Salette Missionaries Newsletter. 2022. https://www.lasalette.org/reflections/faith/1127-vietnam-memorial-helps-veterans-find-healing.html.

had been an Army Chaplain who once celebrated Holy Communion in a field in Vietnam from the hood of a Jeep, singing hymns while carpet bombing occurred on the next ridge over.

"The military experience is different from the civilian experience when it comes to religion," Day said. "In the military, everyone is together. We respect religious differences, but we don't let them divide us. I was a Chaplain in Vietnam and really experienced that, but Fr. Phil, who was infantry and became a priest later, had the same sense. So, we got together, from Catholic to Assemblies of God and everyone in between, and we were bound together by the military experience and our faith involvement, but the difference didn't get in our way. And that characterized Fr. Phil. He was a priest, but he was a priest for everyone. And he loves being a Catholic priest but doesn't let that get in the way."[57]

Despite all these cathectic experiences, there was still a great deal of torment hidden within Fr. Phil's mind in early 1991 after leading a successful conference with the ministers. The thought that Herb Klug had died because of the decision that Fr. Phil had made on March 1, 1970, to attempt a rescue mission, still haunted him. In his heart and mind, Fr. Phil believed that *had we not gone out on that rescue mission, Herb might still be alive today, and I'm the one who made that decision to go out in that field. So, in essence, it's my fault Herb is dead.* Fr. Phil wanted desperately to continue his healing after he returned from his Vietnam trip, but he knew that to do so he would have to confront his feelings of guilt in causing Herb's death.

In June 1991, Fr. Phil received an unexpected call at the VA hospital in Boston from a Vietnam veteran, B.G. Burkett, who wrote a book entitled *Stolen Valor,* about veterans documenting those who either lied about their service in Vietnam or claimed they had received military awards that they did not receive.

"I found out where you worked after I read an article about you in the Vietnam Magazine," the caller said. "Did you really receive the Silver Star?"

"Of course, I did," Fr. Phil countered angrily. "Why would I say that if it wasn't true?"

"A lot of people lie about their service," the caller replied curtly.

Fr. Phil became extremely indignant at the implication and the thought that anyone would dare to think that he would lie about such a thing.

---

[57] Written comments submitted to the authors by Jackson Day. August 2023.

"Calm down, calm down," the caller said sensing Fr. Phil's anger. "I know you are legitimate because I already checked your records through the Freedom of Information Act."

"How dare you? Who the hell do you think you are?" Fr. Phil responded.

"I had every right to do that, and I did," the caller answered. "By the way, have you ever tried contacting Herb Klug's family?"

"I thought about it, but I've never gotten around to doing it. I know they are from Dayton, Ohio, but I have no address and no idea how to get ahold of them," Fr. Phil answered.

"Well, I think you should,"[58] the caller said, ending the phone call as abruptly as he had started it.

Within a week of getting that phone call, Fr. Phil received a letter from the veteran author who had telephoned him the week before. In the letter, the veteran had included the telephone number of Ray Klug in Dayton. Fr. Phil had intended to write the Klugs a letter to introduce himself, but did not want to make a phone call for that purpose. He set the letter aside for nearly two weeks before mustering the courage to make the call.

As he dialed the number, he held one finger on the buttons atop the phone receiver, ready to hang up if someone answered. When a man answered, Fr. Phil's finger froze in position, unable to depress the button that would terminate the call.

"Is this Mr. Klug?" he asked.

"Yes, this is Mr. Klug."

"Did you have a son in Vietnam?"

"Yes, I did."

"Was his name Herb?"

"Yes, what is this about, please?" Ray Klug asked.

"Relax, Mr. Klug. I just wanted you to know that I was with your son when he died. I am a Vietnam veteran who served with him. I would appreciate it if I could just have your address so that I can write you a letter and tell you about what happened. I would also like to go and visit Herb's grave. I would understand if you and your wife didn't want to see me because of the pain that it would cause. My name is Phil Salois and I'm from the Boston area."[59]

---

[58] Authors interview with Fr. Phil Salois, June 16, 2023.
[59] Ibid.

Ray Klug provided his home address and within a week, Fr. Phil had sent him a letter explaining his role in causing Herb's death. He also provided his telephone number and informed the Klugs that he had become a Catholic Priest since the war. He didn't want to shock them later with this revelation in person since they were of a different faith group than him. A short time later, Ray Klug called Fr. Phil to thank him for the letter.

"Thank you for all the information. You are the first person from Herb's unit to contact us in all these years. Mrs. Klug and I would be pleased to meet you when you are ready to come to Dayton, Phil. We will pick you up at the airport and you can stay with us in our home, and we will take you to Herb's grave."[60]

When Fr. Phil discussed this astonishing series of events with others at the VA, they realized how stressful this would be for Fr. Phil and the family of his deceased comrade. They wished the priest well when and if he decided to go, and asked him to relay his experience in the event that other veterans might want to do the same.

In late July, Fr. Phil decided to take an extended weekend and fly to Dayton. At this point in his life, he had never tried to contact any other veterans from his unit, nor did he even know where they lived. He would be alone on the trip to meet the Klugs, and a very nervous and uneasy feeling befell him as he deboarded the plane at the Dayton Airport dressed in civilian clothes. He was greeted by Ray and his wife Beulah Klug and introduced himself simply as Phil Salois.

The car ride from the airport to the Klug's home just outside Dayton was awkward, but once they arrived at their home, Fr. Phil began to open up.

"If I hadn't insisted on going out there to rescue those six men, and Herb hadn't agreed to go with me, he would probably be alive today," he said to Mrs. Klug with a tone of remorse clearly evident in his voice.

"Please don't say that," Beulah replied, "I don't ever want to hear you say that again. I have never blamed you. It was one of those things."[61]

At dinner that evening, Beulah told Fr. Phil that Herb was her son from a previous marriage, and that both she and Herb were abandoned by Herb's biological father when he was very young. She said that Ray came along and sometime later married Beulah and adopted Herb as his own son. Later on, they also had three girls of their own.

---

[60] Ibid.

[61] Ibid.

"Can you tell me what happened after they brought Herb's body back," Phil asked.

"Well, we went to the funeral home and saw him in a casket. They had a glass cover over the casket," she said.

"Why did they do that?" Fr. Phil inquired.

"Because they were afraid I'd try to pick him up."

"What would have been wrong with that?" he probed further.

"Because his arm would have fallen off. Apparently, when they were removing his body and placing it in the helicopter, his arm was severed by enemy fire," she replied.

"I didn't know that. What happened after that in the funeral home?"

"At the wake, the Pastor of our church came down the line toward the casket and said to me, 'Beulah, I'm sorry for your loss. Maybe if you had been going to church more often, God wouldn't have taken your son from you?'"

"Oh, don't tell me that he said that?" Fr. Phil said with a look of anguish on his face. He knew that in the 1970s, many people, including the clergy, were very anti-war. "So, what did you say to him?"

"I said, Pastor, you have a job to do. I expect you to go about your business and do it. And I never went back to the church again."[62]

This had been a long and emotionally draining day for Fr. Phil, and he went to bed early, but not before being told by Ray Klug that they would visit Herb's grave the next day. Fr. Phil spent a restless night in their guest room before joining the Klugs for breakfast the following morning. After serving and eating the meal with them, Beulah suddenly disappeared from the kitchen. Ray said that he would take Fr. Phil to the gravesite, but Beulah would not be going. He claimed that she was not feeling well although Fr. Phil did not detect her illness at breakfast, nor did she mention it.

Herbert Klug sacrificed his life to help Fr. Phil save the lives of five trapped soldiers on that Fateful day in March 1970. He is remembered today as a war hero and recipient of the Distinguished Service Cross. (Photo courtesy of Fr. Phil)

On the way to the cemetery, Fr. Phil asked Ray to stop at a local florist so he could pick up a long-stemmed rose which he wanted to place on Herb's grave. At the gravesite, he knelt down, carefully placed the rose on the grave, and began

---

to speak to Herb. Though he had hoped for a bit of privacy, Ray Klug stood closely behind Fr. Phil and was able to overhear everything that was being said.

"Herb, here I am. I know it's taken me twenty-one years to get here. I'm sorry, but you know you never left me. You've never been away from my heart and my soul. You've been with me in all the ministry I do for the vets, and I want to thank you for the strength that you gave me and for the sacrifice you made for me on March 1. I'll never forget you."[63]

Fr. Phil stood, and as he turned to face Ray Klug, he noticed Ray was crying. Fr. Phil put his arms around him and hugged him.

"Mr. Klug, I'm so sorry that what I said to your son is hurting you."

"No, that's not it at all. It's because I never told my son that I loved him. I was always his disciplinarian, the one punishing him. That's why Beulah isn't here today. I never told her how sorry I was when he died. I don't think she ever knew how much I loved him."[64]

The ride back to the Klug's home was fairly quiet for most of the way, until Fr. Phil broke the silence.

"Mr. Klug, would you like it if I found the guys from the unit who served with Herb, and get them to come to Dayton for a reunion?"

"Oh, yes, I'd love that," Ray said with a glow in his eyes.

* * *

This was the closure that Fr. Phil needed. When he resumed his work at the VA in the Boston area, he was more committed than ever to aiding troubled veterans.

"For me," he would say, "healing is activity. It's doing something. It's not a passive thing. I always tell veterans if you want to be healed, you've got to do something. You can't just sit on your butt and wait for God to heal you. If you know somebody who was killed, try to contact the family, try to visit his grave, try to bring some of your buddies together. That's healing."[65]

Late in 1991, Fr. Phil received news that the family he had sponsored earlier that year from Vietnam, had discretely moved from their apartment in Attleboro, Massachusetts to Santa Ana, California, also known as "Little Saigon" because of the high concentration of Vietnamese peo-

---

[63] Ibid.

[64] Ibid.

[65] Ibid.

ple who settled there. Santa Ana had become like a Vietnamese village with many Vietnamese shops and restaurants scattered throughout. The family had relatives there and the warmer climate was healthier for the husband and wife, both in their sixties. Fr. Phil wished them well and expressed his hope that they would stay in touch.

Meanwhile, Fr. Phil found himself counseling many other veterans and their wives.

"I wasn't just one of the guys anymore," he said. "I was doing a little bit of marriage counseling because a lot of these guys were having troubles with their wives. The wives often did not understand why their husbands were behaving the way they were. And, the husbands weren't communicating with their wives. One party was simply unaware of what the other party was going through. The husbands didn't want to tell the wives anything about Vietnam because they didn't want to hurt them by forcing them to hear the vicious and sometimes inhumane incidents that took place while they were there."[66]

The National Conference of Vietnam Veteran Ministers, true to their commitment at the first Conference in 1990, organized spiritual healing retreats for Vietnam veterans (generally presided over by Reverend Jackson Day) and their spouses and significant others, most often women. According to Rev. Day, the group quickly realized in the discussions that the women were no strangers to trauma, and that they valued the workshops as much as the men.

"Fr. Phil would begin the workshops by telling his trauma story as an invitation and example for others to feel safe in sharing theirs. I did a couple of hours with the group on Saturday mornings that showed Biblical characters they might have been familiar with from childhood who also had their own trauma stories. Fr. Phil was good at encouraging all of us to work together on behalf of the veterans,"[67] Rev. Day said.

* * *

Between November 13th and 18th, 1991, the second National Conference of Vietnam Veteran Ministers took place in Des Plaines, Illinois at a Catholic Retreat Center. Reverend Alan Cutter, a pastor of the Presbyterian Church (USA), had received a letter from a Catholic

---

[66] American Legion Newsletter, A Lifetime of Healing. (Author anonymous) https://www.legion.org/magazine/236274/lifetime-healing.

[67] Comments submitted to the authors by Rev. Jackson Day. August 2023.

priest that had been forwarded to him by a church official. The letter stated that Fr. Phil was seeking members for this new organization of Vietnam veterans who were religious professionals. The requirements for membership were simple: ordination by some group, service in Vietnam as shown by a DD214 (certificate of discharge from Active Duty) and fifty dollars. Rev. Cutter filled out the membership form and joined.

Rev. Cutter had recently moved to Duluth, Minnesota after a ten-year pastorate in West Virginia. He thought a change of scenery might alleviate the attacks of rage, flashbacks, and panic that were becoming more frequent. He had convinced himself that he would be away from the heat and humidity of the south in Duluth and, therefore, could avoid that "trigger" which transported him back to Vietnam. Rarely has someone so blithely stepped, as is said, "from the frying pan into the fire." Duluth had a bus system with diesel buses; the exhaust odor triggered memories of the large trucks in the "ammo trains" in Vietnam. There was a factory that made wood products; their plant emitted an odor that was to Rev. Cutter like the smell of charcoal fires of the towns in Vietnam. So much for a change of venue to get a fresh start.

By then, Rev. Cutter knew that much of his trouble was being caused by what had happened in Vietnam. But, as a religious professional and the one supposed to give assistance to people, he found himself in the uncomfortable position of needing to ask for assistance. He was desperate and in painful turmoil to the point of considering suicide. He needed help. So, one day, around Easter of 1991, he entered the Duluth Veterans Center and introduced himself. Immediately, someone came to speak to him, one of the Veterans Center counselors, a woman named Cindy. She explained to Rev. Cutter that they did not have any free time to talk to him at length that day, but she wouldn't let him leave without making an appointment to come back in a few days. He tried to demur, but Cindy was very persistent.

For Rev. Cutter, this began a long series of one-on-one sessions with Cindy. These appointments were incredibly painful. Bit by bit, Cindy had a way to expose his emotions. After several months of sessions with Cindy, she recommended a twelve-week encounter with a "closed in-country group". It was during this twelve-week period that Fr. Phil's group was meeting in Illinois. Rev. Cutter asked for permission to skip one week with his group to attend the National Conference of Vietnam Veteran Ministers. Permission was granted.

The drive from Duluth to Des Plaines was uneventful. Rev. Cutter arrived a bit late and the evening session had already started. It was a round robin of sharing about who each minister was, when their service was in Vietnam, and where they were now. Rev. Cutter told the group about his Navy service in Vietnam, and explained that he was a patient at the Duluth Veteran Center. Over the next few days, he found himself sheltering his pent-up emotions by drinking heavily after the sessions.

One night, Fr. Phil and the others went out to visit some veterans' organizations. Rev. Cutter stayed back at the retreat center with a dou-ble-amputee marine and an Episcopal priest. They talked and drank for quite a while until Fr. Phil and his group returned. While the others headed for their rooms upstairs, Fr. Phil decided to join Rev. Cutter and one of his drinking mates. All three were quite intoxicated, and when they were finally ready to retire, Fr. Phil suggested they offer a prayer before leaving. The prayer itself was nothing special, but Fr. Phil's closing comments were words that Rev. Cutter would never forget.

"Remember, the only thing we have to give one another is our stories."

The conference was soon ending, and Rev. Cutter still hadn't said much about what was troubling him, what happened in Vietnam. Cutter had earlier given permission for the Duluth Veteran Center to explain to Fr. Phil the program he was involved with at the veteran center. Cindy, the counselor from the center in Duluth, explained to Fr. Phil, himself a VA Chaplain and colleague, that Cutter was clever at using marvelous defenses to hide his true feelings and would Fr. Phil help them in trying to get Cutter to open up a little. "Please send Alan back to us changed," Cindy pleaded to Fr. Phil. Although Fr. Phil had tried to get Rev. Cutter to openly talk about his Vietnam experience, he had had very little suc-cess. So, that evening at supper, he announced that the regular agenda for the meeting that evening would be amended to include a special time of sharing since he felt that not all present had taken advantage of the opportunity to share with the group. Rev. Cutter was fully aware that Fr. Phil's comment was meant for him and he quietly retreated back to his room prior to the start of the 7:30 pm session. Rev. Cutter had thoughts of leaving the conference immediately and he began to pack his things. Then, as if being struck by a lightning bolt, he realized that this type of action was how he always behaved in a crisis, and he decided to stay and tough it out.

When he walked into the meeting at 7:29 pm, everyone was already there and seated, with an opening on the couch for Rev. Cutter between two other people. Fr. Phil had clandestinely asked the others to be in the meeting room at 7:15 pm, where he explained his plan to get Rev. Cutter to open up before the group. The mood was set with dimmed lights and candles, and soft music and songs with a spiritual nature in them, playing in the background.

One member of the group shared something, then another. There was an interlude in which Fr. Phil played another of his chosen selections, this time it was the prayer from *Les Misérables* that included the sentiment "bring him home" and "let him live." Rev. Cutter was writhing on the couch in spiritual agony while this was going on. Then one of the ministers that Fr. Phil had asked to speak did all he could to increase Cutter's discomfort by sharing his own story of fleeing from the horrors.

When the music ended, the room was silent. Fr. Phil looked at Rev. Cutter directly from across the room and merely raised his eyebrows.

"That's it," Cutter said, tossing his glasses down on the table in front of him. He went on, "Let me tell you what happened to the people I was the closest to in Vietnam."

Rev. Cutter honestly believed that he spoke for only a few minutes, while the rest of the group assured him later that he had talked for nearly an hour. He had discussed his loneliness and loss, abandonment, betrayal, and death, the latter caused by his own hand. When he had finished, he was exhausted. He sat back and closed his eyes.

He thought for certain that those in attendance would have found his behavior to be deplorable. When he opened his eyes, there on the table in front of him appeared bread and wine. Together they celebrated the Lord's Supper and Rev. Cutter felt a great sense of personal relief.

The following morning, many from the group wondered how they could help Rev. Cutter going forward. Fr. Phil told them that they had done what they could for Cutter, and that they would know that something good had happened if Cutter showed up at the next conference. He did attend the following year and has not missed one conference in over the twenty years since.[68]

"I will always give Fr. Phil credit for saving my life emotionally," said Rev. Jackson Day at the end of the second Conference. When I came back from Vietnam, I carried a lot of tears I could not express. I felt burnt out in my ministry and entered an alternate career of healthcare project management, which didn't need to engage my emotions. My particulars

---

[68] The information presented on the previous four pages regarding the second National Conference of Vietnam Veteran Ministers held between November 13-18, 1991, was provided on July 1, 2023, by Rev. Alan Cutter, in a written response to questions posed by the authors.

may have been unique, but overall, it was a situation Fr. Phil encountered again and again, and his ministry to veterans was about healing those wounds. At the second conference, Fr. Phil pulled out all the stops. The scriptures were about the pain of coming home. The music was popular song after popular song that all spoke to coming home and not finding what one needed, what one hoped for. It got to me and I ended up crying for over half an hour, tears I had been carrying for decades. After that, my life certainly contained the challenges everyone experiences, but living it was like moving from black and white to color. I will always be grateful to Fr. Phil for that."[69]

* * *

In 1993, the Chief of Chaplains, Reverend Carl Bergstrom, at Jamaica Plain VA decided to retire after a long career. Fr. Phil eagerly applied for the newly vacated position. Having gained recognition and attention within the Veterans Administration, he was elevated to the position of Chief of Chaplains, which carried with it, a significant increase in administrative duties.

That same year, Sister Linda McClenahan, a member of the Racine Dominican Sisters, called Fr. Phil in Boston after reading an ad about a group called the National Conference of Vietnam Veteran Ministers. Their conversation was pleasant albeit strained when Sister Linda heard that she would qualify only as an auxiliary member, as full membership, under the group's current by-laws, was reserved for ordained persons. Her displeasure was further expressed in a follow-up letter that Sister Linda subsequently sent to Fr. Phil declining auxiliary membership. In her letter, the disgruntled nun noted that, as a woman in the Catholic Church, she had already reached the "glass ceiling" as she was barred from ever having the opportunity of ordination, at least in her lifetime. This additional restriction seemed to be an afront to her dedication. She assumed that her letter would terminate discussion of the matter. She closed by wishing the organization well, and never expected to hear from Fr. Phil again.

Fr. Phil, however, was troubled by her quandary. Here was a nun who devoted her entire life to God, and because she wasn't ordained, she would not qualify to become part of a ministers' group. To Fr. Phil, it seemed neither right nor fair. So, he wrote a letter to the membership

[69] Ibid.

explaining Sister Linda's disqualification from becoming a full member, asking if a change to the by-laws was warranted. He petitioned the body to change the requirement for membership to include anyone dedicated for life in the service of their church. The by-laws change was approved, and Sister Linda became a full member of the National Conference of Vietnam Veteran Ministers.

Consequently, at the November 1993 Conference held at the Vista Hotel in Washington, D.C., Fr. Phil dedicated a significant portion of a day to a discussion of women's programs. The theme of a three-hour panel discussion was *Women of Faith/Women of Valor"*, with Fr. Phil moderating a discussion consisting of fifteen panelists. For a copy of the entire women's program, visit Appendix D.

In 1993, after the death of Father Pat Devine, the National Chaplain of the Vietnam Veterans of America, the massive and growing organization sought a replacement to serve in that post. Many in the leadership ranks favored eliminating the position, as they never really supported its creation, but George Duggins, the Vice President of the VVA, was a staunch supporter of replacing the deceased Chaplain, thereby maintaining the position. Fr. Phil's name was placed in nomination, and mainly because he was a Silver Star recipient, he received appointment to a position he has yet to relinquish.

As the incoming National Chaplain, Fr. Phil naturally assumed that he would be asked to deliver the invocation at the 1993 national convention in Norfolk, Virginia. He was mistaken. Instead, the honor was given to a local chaplain. When Fr. Phil entered the convention's main hall, many people were talking. Recognizing one of the voices, Fr. Phil shouted in a surprised tone. "James Edwards?" Without even turning, the man recognized the voice behind him and said, "Phil Salois?" With his southern drawl, the pronunciation was 'Salowis'.

James Edwards was a local Pastor in Norfolk, and the Pastor of the church attended by George Duggins. He was the local pastor that Duggins had chosen to provide the convention's opening prayer. Any resentment that Fr. Phil had harbored as a result of the snub was quickly dissipated. That is because James Edwards was the Lieutenant who "was dropped to us, along with a host of FNGs (F—ng new guys) on March 2nd in Vietnam. "[70] After the war, Edwards entered the seminary and had

---

[70] Authors interview with Fr. Phil Salois, June 16, 2023.

become a Baptist Minister. Seeing him at the convention was an awesome and unexpected reunion.

A few years later, the Veterans Administration considered merging the Jamaica Plain VA with the West Roxbury VA. At the time, the West Roxbury VA was part of the Brockton VA Medical Center with Fr. Henry Nichols as its Chief of Chaplains. Once the merger took place, Fr. Phil found himself applying to become the Chief of Chaplains for the combined VA locations. For that position, he competed with Fr. Nichols. Again, his past combat experience and the Silver Star award placed him above all the other applicants, and Fr. Phil was selected for the position. He now would be splitting his time between Jamaica Plain and West Roxbury, while Fr. Nichols remained in his role as Chief Chaplain of the Brockton VA facility.

* * *

By 1995, Fr. Phil had contacted many of the living members of the Alpha Company veterans with whom he served to determine their interest in holding a company reunion. Interest was high and the men agreed to hold their first reunion in Dayton, Ohio with the Klug family in attendance. The group also decided to hold future bi-annual reunions at different locations every other year.

A total of eleven veterans attended the first reunion in Dayton, including Fr. Phil's good friend, Nick Aragon from New Mexico. Nick had re-enlisted in the Army a few years after the Vietnam War ended, having had trouble adjusting to civilian life. His length of service was enough to earn him a pension, retiring as a Sergeant First Class (E-7). When they went to Herb's grave, LT James Edwards was there, this time in his role as an ordained Baptist Minister. Reverend Edwards had been the one who had replaced LT Terrance Bowell in Vietnam following Bowell's death. He presided over the service held at Herb's grave, while Fr. Phil presided over a second service held at the Vietnam Veterans Memorial located on the Miami River. The river site memorial lists the names of all the deceased men from Dayton who enlisted in the service. Herb's name was on that list.

Half of the veterans attending the reunion were involved in the tragic skirmish of March 1, 1970. The other half were the FNGs, replacement troops who came into the ambush zone on March 2, the day after the rescue. The ceremony at the memorial included an honor guard provided by the veterans of the VVA local Chapter 97, who proudly displayed the colors. Nick Aragon presented Mrs. Klug with a single red rose, saying as he did, "If it weren't for your son and Fr. Phil, I would not be alive today". Mr. Klug and the couple's three daughters, Deborah, Tracy and Nancy, looked on. It was a truly beautiful way to honor their son and brother.

CHAPTER 10

Croatia, Georgia and Colorado

"I have discovered...how powerful and important our
personal stories are to restore us to wholeness and bring us to a
greater sense of inner peace."
Fr. Philip Salois
Vietnam Veterans of America, National Chaplain
In a Speech in Tbilisi, Georgia

Following Alpha Company's first reunion in Dayton, Ohio in 1995, the group decided to hold the second reunion in 1997 in Washington, D.C. Many of the veterans from Fr. Phil's unit attended the reunion.

Fr. Phil was gaining more and more recognition as a counselor for any veteran suffering from PTSD, regardless of the conflict in which the troubled veteran had fought. In early 1998, he was invited to serve on a panel of the First International Conference on the Psycho-Social Consequences of War, organized by the World Veterans Federation held in Dubrovnik, Croatia. He was also asked to present a talk entitled *Journey From Darkness To Light,* a copy of which can be found in Appendix G.

The conference brought together 350 participants from 39 countries of the five continents. The multi-disciplinary orientation of the participants and their geographic span enabled an exchange of views to be held between scientists and clinicians, decision-makers and war veterans and victims of war. This amalgamation of contributors constituted its unique and innovative character.

Fr. Phil was proud and honored to be part of such a prestigious group and confirmed that there was a basis of post-traumatic stress disorder (PTSD) common to war veterans and victims of all armed conflicts and similar situations, regardless of their nature and geographic location. A full copy of the Conference's conclusions is attached in Appendix H.

The World Veterans Federation (WVF) is an international non-profit, non-governmental umbrella veterans' organization founded in the 1950s and headquartered in Paris, France. The organization has over 60 million veteran members across the globe, and its mission is to be the leading organization promoting wellbeing and providing assistance and aid to veterans and victims of war, and assisting the international community in the promotion of international peace and security. The Health and Welfare Division of the WVF has a detailed Veterans Wellbeing Statement, which is available in Appendix I.

Following the April 1998 conference in Croatia, Fr. Phil was even more committed to assisting veterans with PTSD. Throughout his role as the Chief Chaplain at the Jamaica Plain and West Roxbury VA medical centers, he continued to counsel veterans. But there was much more to come.

Members of the National Conference of Vietnam Veteran Ministers all served in that theater of operations and were now ordained ministers. Their common history had taught them that our national experience during the Vietnam War was unlike any other in our history. Out of their own military backgrounds, the members discovered a unique mission in helping guide the search for meaning and spiritual healing for both the veteran community and the nation as a whole.

In partial fulfillment of that mission, the National Conference of Vietnam Veteran Ministers, at the request of Fr. Phil in his capacity as the VVA National Chaplain, developed the VVA Book of Prayers and Services in 1998. The book contains suggested services for use upon the death of a VVA member or VVA Associate, as well as services for Memorial Day or Veterans Day. Fr. Phil spearheaded this effort and was an instrumental member of the Editorial Committee along with the Reverends Jack Day and Alan Cutter.

In 1999, the last VA facility operating on its own in Massachusetts, the Brockton VA Medical Center, was merged with the other two, Jamaica Plain and West Roxbury, forming the VA Boston Healthcare System. Fr. Phil would now be Chief of Chaplain Services for the three major medical centers, a position increasing his responsibilities even more. As his popularity grew, and the respect he gained from other healthcare professionals increased, so did the demand for his time.

During that same period in 1999, likely as a result of veterans who had attended the 1998 Dubrovnik, Croatia conference on PTSD, Fr. Phil was asked to attend and speak to veterans who served in the war

Following the Peaceful Caucasus Conference in Tbilisi, Georgia this book was produced. It contains, in three languages, a transcript of all the presentations given during the conference. (Photo from the book in the collection of Fr. Phil Salois)

in Afghanistan at a Conference entitled Peaceful Caucasus in Tbilisi, Georgia, organized by two human rights activists, Manana Mebuke and Djimal Arkania. He was so well-received that he was invited to Tbilisi and Baku, Azerbaijan to visit their disabled veterans the following year and was even interviewed on a popular radio station program in Baku.

* * *

In the fall of 1999, the Alpha Company reunion was in San Juan Capistrano. It was while there that the group decided to hold its 2000 reunion in Dayton, Ohio, for the second time. That gathering was followed by the 2002 reunion in Littleton, Colorado, just outside Denver. The 2002 event would be the first time Alpha Company visited LT Terrance Bowell's gravesite, thirty-two years after he was killed on that fateful day in Vietnam. The unit hoped to organize a ceremony for the Bowell family similar to the one organized for the Klug family in 1995.

During his tenure as the Chief Chaplain of Services in the VA Boston Healthcare System, Fr. Phil also served as an ad hoc member of the Psychology Department. In an effort to solidify his credentials in counseling veterans with PTSD, he became a Board-Certified Expert in Traumatic Stress (B.C.E.T.S.) in 2001 and received his certificate from the American Academy of Experts in Traumatic Stress.

Since 1989, Fr. Phil had been a resident cleric at the VA Boston Healthcare System, having reached the pinnacle of service as the Chief of Chaplain Services. He continued to work with veterans to help them come to terms with their lives and their faith, often through interdenominational weekend retreats for troubled veterans and their spouses.

"I deal with veterans every day who blame God for the destruction they witnessed, who want God to take the rap for what happened," Fr. Phil noted. "As they retire, a lot of guys have a lot of time on their hands. Their jobs gave them their identity, and with nothing to fall back on, they tend to dwell on the past. We work with them to 'refound' or reconnect with their past by putting their story into a new context that can serve a useful purpose and bring meaning back into their life."[71] PTSD is like a cancer. If untreated, it continues to grow and can lead to a disastrous ending.

* * *

On Sunday, July 28, 2002, the thirty-second anniversary commemoration service for LT Terrance Bowell was held at his gravesite in Fort Logan National Cemetery in Denver, Colorado. Fulfilling their desires, Alpha Company members presented a tribute to Bowell similar to the one that had been given to Herb Klug in 2005. LT Bowell's father, Thomas Bowell of Littleton, Colorado, and the lieutenant's sister, Karen Davis, flew in from Corpus Christi, Texas to attend, along with other members of the Bowell family. A large group of members from Alpha Company participated in the services. Fr. Phil delivered the Opening Prayer and read from the Gospel. This was followed by the recitation of poems, the Laying of a Wreath, and a 21-gun salute. Graveside services also included a presentation of flowers, Honor Awards to family members, and the playing of Taps. All this while bagpipes were reverently played in the background. During this tribute, former PFC Michael Kamrat, a March 1, 1970 survivor who had lost an eye during the rescue attempt, flew his small plane fairly low to the ground as Alpha Company members proudly waved at him. The families were so appreciative of the members of Alpha Company who attended that they hosted a small banquet after the ceremonies.

According to comments left in his loving memory on the website *Find a Grave*, Fr. Phil's immediate superior in Vietnam, Sergeant Kent "Skeeter" Cowel, continues to decorate LT Bowell's grave every Memorial Day.

---

[71] Authors interview with Fr. Phil, June 16, 2023.

CHAPTER 11

U.S. House of Representative

"When one has been exposed to war up close and personal, that person is forever changed, scarred and spiritually wounded."
Fr. Philip Salois
In comments to the U.S. Committee on Veterans' Affairs,
Subcommittee on Health – March 11, 2004

In early 2004, Fr. Phil, in his capacity as the Chief of Chaplain Services at the VA Boston Healthcare System, was asked to speak before the Committee on Veterans' Affairs Subcommittee on Health, in Washington, D.C. The topic was the psycho-spiritual effects on men and women who have participated in, and witnessed first-hand, the horrors of war on the battlefield. The Subcommittee on Health has legislative, oversight, and investigative jurisdiction over the Veterans Health Administration including medical services, medical support and compliance, medical facilities, medical and prosthetic research, and major and minor construction.

Fr. Phil's statement before this House of Representative Subcommittee is included in its entirety.

Statement of
Father Philip G. Salois, M.S.
VISN 1 Chaplain Program manager and Chief, Chaplain Service-VA
Boston Healthcare System
Before the
Subcommittee on Health
Committee on Veterans' Affairs
March 11, 2004

Thank you, Mr. Chairman and Committee Members, for the unique opportunity to be here to address all of you on an important subject very near and dear to my heart – the psycho-spiritual effects on men and women who have participated in and witnessed first-hand the horrors of war on the battlefield.

Let me first of all preface my remarks by giving you a small picture of what qualifies me to speak to the subject. At the age of 20, I was drafted into the United States Army and served as a combat infantryman from 1969-1970. As a result of leading a rescue mission on March 1, 1970, I was awarded a Silver Star. I also served 12 years in the United States Army Reserves as a Chaplain in hospital units; my last assignment was with the 883rd Medical Company (Combat Stress Control). In addition, I have worked for the last 15 years as a Chaplain in the VA Boston Healthcare System with a special focus on PTSD and spiritual healing.

Having gone through an extensive journey of healing myself, and the journey is not over, I can speak as a witness to the fact that when one has been exposed to war up close and personal, that person is forever changed, scarred and spiritually wounded. Even with the best of fore-knowledge and training available, there is absolutely nothing that can prepare a young man or woman for the horrors that war will embed in one's mind, heart and soul. That being said, it is important to learn from lessons from the past, particularly the war in Vietnam and the devastating effects it has had on thousands of men and women. We share the experiences and the wisdom we have gained for our young men and women returning from Iraq and Afghanistan.

The February 15th issue of the *New York Times Magazine* featured a lengthy article "The Permanent Scars of Iraq" by Sara Corbett. It relates the story of a few returning soldiers from the 101st Airborne Division who were wounded both physically and psychologically. Reading this article transported me back some 30-plus years as something that could have been written in the 70s, only the characters and geography have changed.

Sleepless nights…nightmares…flashbacks…self-medicating with al-cohol and drugs…not communicating with the spouse…thousand-yard stare, and the saga rages on. The psychosocial-spirited effects of war are universal as I learned when I met war veterans from all over the world at the First International Conference of Psycho-Social Consequences of War in Dubrovnik, Croatia in April 1998. There is a common denomina-tor among persons who have engaged in hostile fire in time of war, and that common denominator is deep-seated wounds at every human level. The memory is forever branded into the fabric of one's life.

How do we meet the challenge of reaching out to our brother and sister veterans who have been to hell and come back to talk about it? It is often said in the circle of ministers I associate with that, "Religion is for those afraid of hell…and spirituality is for those who have been there and don't want to go back!"

Veterans Affairs Chaplains are certified and clinically trained to serve the spiritual needs of the returning veterans from Iraq and Afghanistan. It is of paramount importance that VA Chaplains play an integral role on the mental health inter-disciplinary teams in our medical facilities. They continue to provide excellent one-on-one spiritual and pastoral counseling to our veteran patients. They also facilitate spirituality groups for those suffering from PTSD and substance abuse. In fact, there are two 12-step models that have been drafted with a special focus on PTSD modeled after the 12-steps of Alcoholics Anonymous.

In 1989, I founded the National Conference of Vietnam Veteran Ministers, an organization comprised of people like myself who served in Vietnam as enlisted men and women and later answered the call to ordained ministry. We also invited Vietnam Chaplains to join. The purpose was to share our trauma stories with one another on the level of faith and spirituality so that we could receive affirmation and healing of our souls. It truly was and still is a clinic for wounded PTSD-ridden ministers. As an outgrowth of this organization, which is better referred to as a community, we began to explore ways of sharing our stories with combat veterans. Combat veterans, by the very nature of their exposure to battle, i.e., killing and witnessing death, develop a poisonous world-view causing a wounded "Imago Dei." This phrase, "Imago Dei," or Image of God, refers to the belief that all persons are created in God's image.

That wounded "Imago Dei" is characterized by secret-keeping, loss of voice and self-enforced separation. Secret-keeping…how can I ever talk about what I witnessed and participated in on the battlefield to my spouse, my children, my friends? As a result, this causes us to lose our voice. If we are keeping secrets, then we stop communicating, which then forces the third factor…self-enforced separation, isolation, or more commonly referred to as "bunkering in." Our combat veterans experience deep guilt, which comes in many forms: guilt from killing or maiming civilians, children who may be booby-trapped or enemies disguised as friendlies. It could be guilt over a mistake, which caused the mutilation or death of a comrade. It could be guilt over being a survivor when buddies were killed. The list goes on.

One way the National Conference of Vietnam Veteran Ministers found to be helpful was to develop a Spiritual Healing Weekend Retreat program for combat veterans and their spouses or significant others. In the past seven years, we have offered 15 of these retreats throughout the country. Although it is a mere drop in the bucket, veterans and their families have been greatly comforted and assisted spiritually in these retreats. Many couples have come back to these retreats and brought other couples with them. We felt it was important to try to get the veteran to bring their spouse or significant other to these retreats, because our goal was to help heal the family and not just the veteran…to re-open those doors of communication, the lack of which can destroy a relationship.

The main point I want to make before this committee is the importance of making the combat veteran, particularly those who are now coming home from overseas deployment, begin the process of telling their story to someone who can encourage them and guide them in a healing, loving and accepting manner. They may feel they are "damaged goods." The role of the Chaplain is to help them recognize that their experience offers them a unique perspective on the meaning of life and that their suffering is not meaningless, but can be redemptive. The Chaplain can help the veteran learn what it means to be a "wounded healer"-which the veteran in his or her woundedness can help heal another wounded veteran.

That is the gift of life one person can give to another. The theory of the Sacred Story we teach them is the use of their personal story as a vehicle for healing. The development of one's unique story through eyes of faith and ultimately the redemptive value of their Sacred Story can move them from a state of being "scared," recognizing that they are "scarred," and ultimately seeing themselves as "sacred." It is a far greater task for the minister to guide the veteran in this direction than moving letters around in a word-play, but it gets the point across. We tell our veterans that there is no one else on earth like them, just as there are not two fingerprints the same, neither is their story. It is a true gift of love when they can speak the story with all the trauma, pain, suffering, tears and emotions, and share that story with another human being who is hurting.

Over the years, I cannot count how many Vietnam veterans and veterans from World War II and Korea I have counseled, but the end result of war and its impact on our psyche is the same. I, along with my colleagues, welcome the opportunity to reach out to the returning soldiers, marines, sailors and airmen and women to begin that healing process so that it does not begin to fester and grow like a cancer that eats away at the core of their being. If we knew back in the 70s and 80s what we know today, how many lives could have been saved? How many marriages could have been saved? Who knows?

Thank you once again for the opportunity to address this esteemed body.

Father Philip G. Salois, M.S.

CHAPTER 12

PTSD Goes on and Fr. Phil loses a Good Buddy

"Had it not been for your son and Phil, I would not be standing in front of you. I am here because of what Herb and Phil did, and for that I will always be grateful."

Nick Aragon, 2nd Platoon, New Mexico

During the following years, Fr. Phil continued to attend biennial reunions with his combat buddies. Each reunion was held in a different city each time they met. Similar annual conferences were also held by the newly formed International Conference of Veteran Ministers that now encompassed ministers from other countries, and conflicts other than those fought in Vietnam.

Fr. Phil continued to focus his attention on cases of PTSD at the Boston VA Healthcare System. Now, however, those cases also included veterans suffering from PTSD resulting from tours of duty in Iraq and Afghanistan.

It is natural to experience feelings of fear during and after a traumatic situation. Fear is part of the body's "fight-or-flight" response, which helps veterans avoid or appropriately respond to potential danger. Veterans may experience a range of reactions after trauma, and most people recover from initial symptoms over time. Those who continue to experience problems may be diagnosed with PTSD.

People who have PTSD may feel stressed or frightened, even when they are not in danger. But not everyone with PTSD has been through a dangerous event. Sometimes, learning that a friend or family member experienced trauma can cause PTSD. This phenomenon, referred to as secondary PTSD, is frequently endured by wives and children of returning combat veterans.

According to the *National Center for PTSD,* a program of the U.S. Department of Veterans Affairs, about six out of every one hundred people will experience PTSD at some point in their lives. Women are more likely to develop this condition than are men. In addition, certain aspects of the traumatic event, and specific biological factors (such as genes) may make some people more likely to develop PTSD.

In 2005, during the war in Iraq, members of the 883rd Medical Company headed to that country for a second deployment. The unit, made up of psychiatrists, psychologists, social workers and other mental health workers, was trying to ease the stress for soldiers on the front lines of battle in Iraq. The 'combat stress control' unit went where the soldiers were, into their tents, dining halls and chapels to offer counseling advice and sometimes would patiently listen to a soldier who might be suffering from anxiety, depression, insomnia and a host of other psychological problems associated with combat.

"For many years I saw March 1 as doomsday," Fr. Phil would later say. "Now I have a celebration in honor of that day. I've got another buddy who lives nearby. He was in the 4th Infantry Division, and that same week he had nine of his guys killed. We try to get together with some other guys and go to dinner, and we celebrate. We toast these men that we lost. I think and talk about it a lot, because it's made me who I am today. If I hadn't gone to Vietnam, I don't know where I'd be."[72]

*   *   *

Time marched on, as did Phil's work at the VA hospital. By the time 2009 came along, Fr. Phil had counseled nearly a hundred veterans. He did not seek recognition for his efforts, but it came his way nevertheless. In 2010, he was selected to be one of seventy Commissioners on the 'Truth Commission for the 'Conscience in War' Conference held in New York City. He was part of a select gathering to launch a major nationwide conversation about freedom of conscience for members of our nation's armed forces. The result was the publishing of a white paper for the Department of Defense on the subject of morality of war and conscientious objection to wars deemed immoral.

"It was an interesting mix of people attending. I am looking forward to this ongoing experience," Fr. Phil noted at the time.

By 2012, *USA Today* reported that fifty thousand new veterans were

---

72 American Legion Newsletter, A Lifetime of Healing. February 23, 2017.

diagnosed with PTSD, and sixty-five hundred veterans released from military service had taken their own lives.

"Part of the problem is that in large part, Iraq and Afghanistan war veterans have been on multiple tours. That just kind of wears on them. It becomes almost a lifestyle for them. Veterans now often come home feeling unaccepted by their families. And they carry a lot of secrets, things they were involved in, people that they've lost, seeing death and destruction. For many of these young people, that's the first time they've encountered death, or contributed to killing. So, they come back with a lot of shame, a lot of guilt, survivor guilt. Why did I survive when my buddy was killed?" Fr. Phil said.

Once a clinician determined that a veteran was struggling with spiritual issues, Fr. Phil stepped in for counseling. He explained that he saw two basic groups of veterans; the first are those who are in the National Guard and the Reserves. Those people tend to be older, family-oriented people who seem more likely to have some kind of spiritual base. The second group tends to be comprised of younger veterans who are "unchurched". Communication with people from this group is much more difficult.

"Not all patients are willing or ready to speak with a religious professional," Fr. Phil noted. "Unchurched youth are difficult to speak to on religious, spiritual terms. It's more of what you get from the internet or from New Age stuff. It's very hard for us old-timers to find a language that they can understand. So, I basically talk to them about values, about their morals and what they were brought up with. Many have grown up in broken homes and lacked a father figure. In fact, that's why many of them entered the military. After the military service, there's nothing for them to come back to. They can't find jobs because the things the Army or the Marines taught them are not very useful in civilian life." Spiritual healing takes time, perhaps even more than physical convalescence.

"It's going to take a while for them to talk," Fr. Phil said of those who are mentally, spiritually, or emotionally hurt. They don't trust people; they only trust their buddies that they serve with. So, they come back to civilian life and speak to a civilian who more than likely doesn't understand what they're talking about, only what they've learned in books or from talking to other veterans. So, I talk to them about forgiveness and reconciliation. That comes at the end of a long process," he added.

"Retreats are available to veterans struggling with spiritual issues, but in many cases, those leading those retreats need to be able to speak to an unchurched generation. We try to use a lot of symbols, like writing the name of your buddy on a piece of paper in remembrance of him, and at the end of a service we burn all these papers and let the smoke rise to heaven, perhaps add a little incense with it, and explain to them that maybe that's a symbol of their spirit rising to God. These kids are very visual people, so if you can give them a spiritual symbol as a sign of God, it makes it easier to understand."[73]

*   *   *

The 2012 Alpha company reunion was held in Durango, Colorado. Nick Aragon, one of the men Fr. Phil had rescued on March 1, 1970, forty-two years earlier, and a good friend of his, attended that reunion. Most of the men there were now in their early sixties. Nick was sixty-two. It was a sad occasion for Nick as he announced to the group that he had been diagnosed with Stage 4 stomach cancer, and had only a few months to live.

"I wanted to see you all for one more time," Nick said. As an aside in a quiet moment during the reunion, Nick confronted Fr. Phil.

"When I die, Phil, would you please come and celebrate my Funeral Mass?" he asked.

"Of course, Nick. I'll be there,"[74] Fr. Phil answered with a shadow of sadness overtaking his face.

On November 2, 2012, just a few months following the reunion. Fr. Phil received a telephone call from Nick's daughter, Selene Aragon, informing him of Nick's death just four days shy of his sixty-third birthday. The Mass of Christian Burial would be celebrated on November 5th at Our Lady of the Light Catholic Church in Cubero, New Mexico, she told him. Fr. Phil immediately booked a flight to Albuquerque.

As Fr. Phil began the Noontime celebration of the Mass at the little chapel on an Indian reservation, he thought to himself, *these people are probably wondering who was he to come here to celebrate the funeral Mass of their beloved friend and family member?* When Fr. Phil rose to give the homily at the Mass, he explained to them the story of how he and Nick met in Vietnam forty-two years earlier, and described the events of March 1, 1970, and all the reunions they had attended in between. Suddenly, the funeral service in general, and Fr. Phil's homily in particular became a healing moment for the community who knew Nick, and for the family

---

[73] Burger, John, The Catholic Report, The Longest Battle. May 6, 2014.

[74] Authors interview with Fr. Phil Salois, June 16, 2023.

The highly decorated Nick Aragon died on October 28, 2012, and is interred at Cubero Cemetery on the Indian Reservation in New Mexico. (Photo from the Internet site Find A Grave)

who loved him. Many of Nick's family members and friends wept. They were comforted in the knowledge that Nick no longer suffered and was finally at rest, physically, mentally and spiritually. Nick Aragon, a recipient of the Silver Star, the Bronze Star and the Purple Heart, was interred with full military honors at Cubero Cemetery on the Indian reservation.

CHAPTER 13

Fairwell to Two of My Loves

While 2012 drew to a close on a sad note with the death and burial of Fr. Phil's good friend, Nick Aragon, the early part of 2013 held out even less hope for joy. On March 20, Fr. Phil lost his best friend when his mother Hélène suffered a massive stroke and succumbed just two days later on March 22nd at the age of 84. Fr. Phil was devastated by the sudden and unexpected loss of the one person to whom he felt closest throughout his entire life.

Sometime before her passing, perhaps in anticipation of her own death, Hélène had asked her son to make three promises to her: First, that her body not be cremated after her death; Second, that she never wanted to be placed in a nursing home; and Third, that she be buried alongside her late husband, Walter, at the Riverside National Cemetery in Riverside, California. Fr. Phil had visited her during these last two days, and she told him "I want to go home." Fr. Phil knew what she meant. She wanted to go home to God and to her husband.

On March 20, 2013, Hélène Salois, Fr. Phil's best friend and mother, joined her husband Walter in the presence of God. She was 84 years old. (Photo courtesy of Fr. Phil Salois)

Hélène Salois' Mass of Christian Burial was celebrated on March 27, the Wednesday of Holy Week, at Our Lady Queen of Martyrs Church in Woonsocket. But, as he had promised, Fr. Phil flew to California with her remains on April 1ˢᵗ, the day after Easter, where she was interred alongside her husband at the Riverside Cemetery.

Fr. Phil soon moved from his apartment in Newtonville, Massachusetts to his mother's home of thirty years, a small ranch home in North Smithfield, Rhode Island. The priest realized that moving into his mother's home would bring with it an outpouring of emotions, but he also believed that her spirit within those walls would introduce a remarkable sense of calm and comfort. "I knew from the day Mom bought the house that it would be mine when she died," Fr. Phil noted. So, when that day arrived, it signaled the end of apartment living for him. "As sad as it was, I knew that Mom wanted me to have the house, and so knowing that, and [knowing] that her spirit was still in the house and still is to this day," had a calming effect. He explained with tongue in cheek that at times items left in a certain place will be found in a different location within the house. "I think she is letting me know she is still here smiling down at me. There are so many other coincidences that happened...I know she is here fooling with me," he observed.

In early January 2014, Fr. Phil was named Veteran of the Year for 2014 by the United Veterans Council of Woonsocket, Rhode Island. The Council's selection was based on Fr. Salois' lifelong work to help Vietnam veterans and their families overcome the trauma that resulted from combat and loss of life. He was nominated by the Lincoln, Rhode Island Vietnam Veterans' Post 818. On January 21 of that same year, a resolution was introduced into both the Senate and the House of the Rhode Island General Assembly congratulating him on being named 2014 Veteran of the Year, a copy of the Joint Resolution can be found in Appendix L.

Fr. Phil was now sixty-five years old. When he first accepted a position at the Jamaica Plain VA in late 1989, he was only forty-one. The day-to-day stress and the constant demand for his ministerial services over these past twenty-four years had begun to take its toll on Fr. Phil's health, and thoughts of retirement started to flood his mind.

A next generation of Chaplain would soon be needed. So long as there were conflicts involving soldiers in battle, there would be a need for spiritual counselors when these young warriors returned home to a completely new and different life as a civilian. And for the new generation of military Chaplains out in the field, it was clear that "without the priest, there are no sacraments; there's no experience of the

Church for the soldiers."[75] One need only trace the roots of chaplaincy, an institution deeply ingrained in our military history, to realize the veracity of that statement. "One of President George Washington's first actions as a leader of this great nation was to ask for Chaplains…since the very beginning of the military service in the United States, we've had Chaplains,"[76] according to Ryan Scheel on a captivating episode of *The Catholic Talk Show.*

On February 28, 2015, Fr. Phil officially retired as Chief of Chaplain Services at the Boston VA Healthcare Systems, a position he had held for twenty-three years. He had counseled at length over a hundred veterans and their families during this time, and had created spiritual retreats, conferences, and various work sessions, all in the name of spiritual healing for veterans and veterans who entered a ministry following their experiences in conflicts. He had received a long list of military awards besides the Silver Star, had been awarded numerous and prestigious clergy awards, and still continued to receive accolades for his service as a Chaplain and counselor to veterans returning home from conflicts in Vietnam, Iraq and Afghanistan.

A scrawny, curly-haired redhead infantryman, barely twenty years old, had answered the call to both God and country after making a promise in 1970, and forty-five years later could confidently say that he had kept that promise. So, he was calling it a day…or was he?

Fr. Phil would not disappear from active life just yet. He kept his role as the National Chaplain of the Vietnam Veterans of America, having out served five national VVA Presidents along the way.

In 2019, Fr. Phil was appointed the National Chaplain of the American Legion, another post he still retains today. On February 27th of that year, he was asked by U.S. Representative David Cicilline (D-RI) to be the Guest Chaplain at the opening session of the United States House of Representatives. In his opening prayer before Congress on that day, Fr. Phil asked God for a spirit of peace and harmony in times of disagreement, and the ability of our leaders to compromise in the enactment of beneficial solutions to our nation's problems. Above all, he prayed for the protection and safe return of all those in uniform who are defending our country. Fr. Phil concluded his prayer asking for special

---

[75] Ryan, George, ChurchPop, The Invisible Battlefield: How Military Chaplains are Fighting the Spiritual War. July 16, 2023.

[76] Ibid.

remembrance of "those who are held prisoner in foreign lands, those missing in action, as we continue to seek them out and bring them home to their loved ones."[77]

In his introduction of Fr. Phil, Congressman Cicilline said: "Madam Speaker, I rise today to recognize Father Philip Salois, who delivered today's opening prayer.

Father Phil is a native of Woonsocket, Rhode Island, and now lives in North Smithfield, Rhode Island, a community that I am proud to represent today in Congress. He served our country in uniform during the Vietnam war as a combat Infantryman and earned the Silver Star for his valor. After his service to our country, Father Phil felt called to service in another capacity. He was ordained into the priesthood on June 10, 1984. A few years later, Father Phil joined the Veterans Administration in Boston, where he served as chief of the chaplain service from 1993 to 2015. Today, he continues to minister to veterans in Rhode Island and all across America. We owe all of our service members and their families an incredible debt of gratitude. The men and women of the United States Armed Forces represent our Country's most important values of service, honor, courage, and sacrifice. This is especially true of Father Phil, who represents the very best of our country and my home State of Rhode Island. I thank him for his service to our country and for being here today to offer the beautiful opening prayer. We are truly honored by his presence."[78]

The full transcript of this segment of the February 27, 2019 Congressional Record can be found in Appendix J.

---

[77] Excerpt from the prayer of Fr. Philip Salois who served as guest chaplain for US House of Representatives to open the 2019 session of February 27, 2019.

[78] Remarks of Congressman David Cicilline (D-RI) in his introduction of Fr. Phil Salois, the Chaplain who delivered the opening prayer before Congress. Congressional Record, February 27, 2019.

CHAPTER 14

I Kept My Promise

"Thank you for all you've done for all Vietnam vets.
As far as I can tell, I think you've more than fulfilled your
promise to God.

Kammy McCleary
Red Cross Worker and Donut Doll
Vietnam

"I have often reflected on how many blessings I have received," Fr. Phil said in an April 2023, "particularly in my ministerial life working with veterans in the VA Hospital systems, in my local community, and even with international war veterans. I have truly lived a blessed life and I give thanks to God for calling me back in 1975."[79]

Many people make solemn promises to God when they find themselves in distress or in a time of need, and it's almost a cliché to say that many soldiers have prayed to God to keep them safe during battle; it is a natural thing to do. But how many of those soldiers actually remember the promise they made when they were under extreme periods of stress? Perhaps more importantly, how many actually follow through on that promise once the cause of that stress has subsided?

Fr. Phil appeared at first to be no different than the many other young soldiers who prayed for survival, or to emerge unharmed during an engagement with the enemy. In fact, four years after leaving Vietnam, the promise he made to God was buried somewhere in his memory like so many unpleasant experiences from that distant land. In his mind, the promise he made was not even a consideration when he entered the seminary. Rather, the desires of that young veteran who

---

[79] Lennon, Frank, Providence Journal, Promise Kept. April 17, 2023

entertained thoughts of becoming a priest were not remotely connected to the promise made on the battlefield in 1970. At the time, Phil Salois genuinely thought his calling to the priesthood was his destiny. The locution, that inner voice he heard that summer day in 1975 while walking in the fields overlooking St. John's Seminary in California, reminded him for the first time since returning home, of the promise he made four years earlier in the jungles of Vietnam. Some might think it was a coincidence that Phil was already preparing for the priesthood when God spoke to him that day. Others might call it destiny. Either way, God's message to Phil was quite clear. God intended for Phil to become a priest.

It was only a few years after being ordained with the La Salette Missionary Order in 1984 that Fr. Phil realized what was intended for him when God said, "This is what I want you to do." Fr. Phil began working only a single day a week with veterans in the Providence VA hospital, but that schedule grew subsequently into a ministry that consumed five days a week. That ministry, in turn, continued to expand, until he became the Chief of Chaplain Services for the entire Boston VA Health Systems counseling veteran after veteran, and their families, along the way.

As if that wasn't enough, Fr. Phil organized counseling programs for other ministers who also served in some branch of our nation's military. He did so not only here in the United States, but all over the world. Chapter fifteen contains first-hand accounts from former soldiers, military chaplains, cohorts in veterans' organizations, and dozens of veterans who desperately needed PTSD counseling for the mental and physical trauma caused them by the horrors that wars create. These former soldiers come from various countries like Georgia, Croatia, Australia, the United Kingdom, Ireland and beyond, and they all deliver the same message, "There is help for the spiritual ills that trouble you. You are not alone."[80]

PTSD raises its ugly head from time to time, even for veterans who have successfully undergone extensive counseling to rid themselves of this affliction. But the ability to learn to cope with it has enabled thousands of veterans to lead productive, normal lives over the years. Fr. Phil did not realize back in 1975 that this was what God had intended for him to do. And he never lost his focus along the way.

---

[80] Fr. Philip Salois, Interviewed by the authors, May 26, 2023.

Fr. Phil has made a habit of making some of the loneliest veterans feel special and wanted. Here he is greeting a fellow Vietnam Veteran with a warm embrace. (Internet photo)

Suddenly, as if out of nowhere, he was sixty-seven years old, and his body was telling him that the daily commute from his home in North Smithfield, Rhode Island to the hospitals in Boston, Massachusetts was taking its toll. "As I look back on my life," Fr. Phil said in a recent interview with the authors, "I feel like I am so tired. I'm exhausted. It's because I expended a lot of energy in my midlife, you know, my 40s and my 50s, and now I'm slowing down...and it's okay, I can give myself permission to do that."

Coupled with his fatigue and overall feeling of being "burnt out," Fr. Phil faced another dilemma, one which perhaps constituted the most difficult decision that he ever had to make. After forty-five years of professed life with the Missionaries of La Salette, the order wanted Fr. Phil to take on a different assignment. Accepting the new challenge would mean leaving a ministry to the local veterans of Rhode Island. Having spent the last thirty-four years of his life helping those veterans find theirs, this was something he just didn't want to do. Accepting the new assignment would also mean that he would have to sell his house, packed with so many memories and perhaps the spirit of his mom, and do so within just two weeks. That wouldn't even have allowed him a sufficient opportunity to look through all those boxes of memories that were stored throughout his home. These were requests that the aging and tired priest was just not willing to accept.

He understood that his refusal would unlock a chain of events that would lead to his ultimate dismissal from the order, but it was a consequence that he would just have to accept.

So, the daily routine at the Boston VA Health Systems ended in his forced retirement in 2015. Fr. Phil is no longer a member of the La Salette Community. He can no longer celebrate any public Masses or perform any function involving the Sacraments of the Catholic

Fr. Phil in the home of his fellow Vietnam Veteran friend Albert "Bert" Guarnieri in North Providence, Rhode Island. (Photo courtesy of Fr. Phil Salois)

Church in public. However, he remains an ordained Catholic Priest. That is for life. And, his work with local veterans in the American Legion continues, so much so that in 2019, at age seventy-one, he became the National Chaplain of the American Legion. In addition, he continues to serve as the National Chaplain of the Vietnam Veterans of America.

As a young and gallant infantryman in a moment of desperation, Phil Salois was faced with a decision. The decision he made would eventually change the course of his life. In return for the grace God bestowed on him that day, one young soldier promised to do anything that God wanted.

Fr. Philip G. Salois kept that promise!

CHAPTER 15

One Man's Impact on the Nation

"I found this man not only a true friend, but also an interesting versatile personality, with a kind and magical character. His charisma and determination conquered me."

Michael Tsikaridze, Georgian Veterans Federation

Chapters 15 and 16 provide a small glimpse of the esteem with which Fr. Phil is held throughout the United States of America and the world. These chapters contain thoughts shared by people with whom he served in Vietnam, those with whom he worked at the VA and other veterans' organizations, and those he helped heal mentally and spiritually along the way through his counseling efforts.

This is by no means an exhaustive list of people whose lives have been touched by this hero priest. Even just a one-paragraph statement from all the people Fr. Phil has aided could occupy an entire book. Rather, the statements contained in chapter 15 written by those impacted by Fr. Phil here at home in the United States, and those found in chapter 16 penned by people changed by him abroad, are just a few that were sought and selected for inclusion in this book.

The testimonials from people that Fr. Phil has affected through his ministerial work, in this country and abroad, make abundantly clear the positive and life-altering impact that he has had on the lives of so many people. These testimonials are uncensored and untouched and reflect the true and innermost feelings of many others throughout the world.

Thank you for all you've done for all Vietnam vets. As far as I can tell, I think you've more than fulfilled your promise to God.

Kammy McCleary
Donut Doll in Vietnam
Red Cross Worker, part of Red Cross Supplemental
Recreational Activities Overseas (SRAO) Program

Phil was and is a good soldier, and when I attended a reunion about 30 years ago in Colorado, I was surprised to see Phil had become a priest. Phil and I served in Vietnam from January 1970 until September 1970, when the unit was sent home and Phil had the honor of returning with the colors.

Vincent Boscia
Always Alpha Group
A/3/7 2nd Platoon

Father Phil is a true example of a veteran's veteran.

Retired Air Force Brigadier Gen. James D'Agostino
West Greenwich, RI

I had heard stories of Phil and others that my husband served with in Vietnam through the years. I was finally able to meet Phil in Dayton, Ohio in 1995. I can't remember now what I had envisioned him to be like, it was nearly 30 years ago since then, but I was introduced to this rotund man dressed in khaki shorts, a Hawaiian shirt, and rope sandals. No priestly presence evident. I adored him from the beginning, and he has been my friend ever since. He has been such a supporter of what now is Always Alpha. He is always ready to serve as a priest and comrade to all of us. Phil and I sneak off together and enjoy a martini and a little conversation whenever we come together. It is an honor to know him.

Gretchen Cowel
Wife of former Sergeant Kent "Skeeter" Cowel

In 1969-70, my memories of Phil, who I called by his last name, while mispronouncing it, was that of a skinny little red-haired kid who was new to the unit, and I didn't put much stock in him. That must have been part of the reason I was so amazed at the bravery I witnessed on March 1st. I think of that day every day!

During the ambush, I was shot in the leg and was told by a medic I'd be leaving on the next helicopter. I noticed Phil Salois and Herb Klug deep in conversation near a huge boulder. A little while later, the shooting intensified and I noticed that both of them were no longer there. What I did notice was the sound of the M-79 grenade launcher going off with an amazing frequency. I carried that weapon for a while, so I know that Salois was working very hard. I even turned to someone and, in amazement, said "That's Salois out there." Later, at the hospital in Saigon, I talked to Lt. Hoover about Salois and what I knew he was doing. I asked that he be recognized for his action. I had not realized that Herb Klug had gone out with him. Herb Klug was killed that day as was my Lieutenant, Terry Bowell. My admiration for Phil Salois will never wane.

Former Sergeant Kent "Skeeter" Cowel
2nd Platoon

I served with Phil in Vietnam in 1969-1970. I was in the 1st Platoon, so I was not close to Phil at that time. I do remember him and will always remember his "boyish" look. I've gotten together with Phil a number of times over the past 15 years and I am proud to call him my friend. Phil is well-known for keeping his promise to serve God, a promise that I believe most grunts make during combat. I know that I did. Phil's story is a great one!

David "Chucky" McKee
1st Platoon

The narrative of the relationship I have had with Phil has never been static or boring. From that Second Conference of Vietnam Ministers when he ambushed me, through all the other conferences we attended, and the retreats we co-led, he always seemed to be challenging and encouraging me to take the next risk, the next step on an uncertain journey that offered the chance of hope and healing. I tried to do the same for him. We followed different paths, as our backgrounds, personalities, and military experiences were quite different. There were ups and downs over the years, and we disagreed and irritated each other, but we trusted each other for comfort in times of distress. Our shared wish and commitment to helping veterans escape the crushing loneliness and silence that has burdened warriors over the centuries bound us together as companions. Over the years, our own stories grew and grew. We learned that the mystery of God's grace is revealed when we share our stories of joy and sorrows, tales full of laughter and tears. Furthermore, that Phil and I can embrace each other with the strange respect and love that only warriors know is proof that God has a terrific sense of humor.

Rev. Dr. Alan Cutter
Retired Pastor of the Presbyterian Church (USA)

My best friend in Vietnam was a Massachusetts woman named Linda Bracket Grasso. She finally came to a few retreats that were held for veterans, but would never tell her story. One year she promised she would talk at the next retreat, but she died in June that year. Phil, after offering sympathy, laughed and said, "Just like her to die so she wouldn't have to share her story!" This made me laugh, too. Father Phil presided at her funeral, and at the grave service. He doesn't know this, but as everyone was leaving the cemetery, and I remained with Linda by myself for a bit, I overheard a couple of Military guard members present say, "Did you get a load of that 'fat, old Priest?" and they laughed. I blew up at them and said, "That fat, old priest was awarded the Silver Star in Vietnam for saving lives after his combat unit, the 199th Infantry, was caught in a horseshoe ambush, an action during which his best friend was killed. He was more 'bad-ass' than you wusses can ever hope to be. And now he works diligently with veterans all over the country helping them sort out their own traumas." They apologized to me, and I said, "You never know what someone has gone through, or has done in their lives, snap judgements are morally wrong. Remember that."

Sister Linda J. McClenahan, "Sister Sarge"
Member of the Racine (WI) Dominican Sisters
Licensed counselor in PTSD
Former Staff Sergeant, 1st Signal Brigade, Long Binh

Father Phil has been and remains a great and inspiring figure.

Jan Scruggs
Founder of the Vietnam War Veterans Memorial Wall
Washington, D.C.

In 1995, Fr. Phil and some of the guys from their unit came to Dayton to pay their respects to my brother Herb, twenty-five years after his death. Fr. Phil and my brother served together in the Army during the Vietnam

War. After being ambushed during a mission, Fr. Phil and my brother went out looking for their wounded buddies. My brother was killed by a rocket grenade that March 1, 1970. When my brother was killed, it was so devastating to all of us. I feel like my mom and dad, talking to these guys, helped them with their grief. Herb was the greatest brother anyone could have ever asked for.

Fr. Phil will always hold a special place in our hearts.
Tracy Klug Frecker
sister of Herb Klug

We really didn't know what a gem we had in Father Salois. I knew he was a Vietnam veteran, but during my pastoral visits to the VA Medical Centers in Boston, he never talked about his experiences in Southeast Asia. I suspected he was suffering from PTSD, and I knew he was involved in numerous Veterans organizations. What I did not know at the time was that he earned a Silver Star in recognition of his bravery in combat. That distinction gave him instant credibility in his exchanges with fellow veterans, patients, medical center staff and chaplains throughout his career. I knew Father Phil was devoted to his elderly mother and spent as much time as possible caring for her. He enjoyed an outstanding reputation in the Archdiocese for the Military Services and among the chaplains of the Department of Veterans Affairs, and was widely known as a gifted counselor and mentor. To this day, Father Phil oozes compassion and empathy and continues to minister to fellow veterans and their families. Besides his extraordinary talents and experience, Father Phil just happens to be a very holy man! It was a privilege to serve with him.

Most Reverend Richard Higgins
Auxiliary Bishop Emeritus
Archdiocese for the Military Services, USA
Former Vicar for Veterans Affairs

I can never truly appreciate the limitless hazards in the life of a Grunt who struggles daily just to survive the Vietnam War.

I am an Army Nurse who was stationed in the relative safety and security of the 12th EVAC Hospital, Operating Room in Cu Chi, Republic of Vietnam. I do however appreciate the sound of 25 ID base camp in-coming and the response of outgoing fire, but I never will truly 'know" what in-coming must have sounded like, crushing oneself deeper into the very earth, as much as humanly possible to be safe in the dark of night when Charlie rules the land.

The fear was there all the days and sleepless nights In-country, whether in Base Camp, walking point in the Boonies on a Search and Destroy Mission, having had to leap from the constantly flying Chopper insertion into a hot LZ with pumping mega-Adrenalin and Cortisol amounts into each and every super-saturated cell in one's body.

How can a woman understand the unremitting blazing heat of 120 degrees or the ultimate fatigue, the all too brief rest of taking a cigarette break, or a swift wiping of one's perpetually sweaty drenched face with the one, each, OD green towel hung around one's neck, but realizing one can never be dry of the sweat or heat of the jungle, the perpetually smelling of saturated wet fatigues and boots, the incredibly too small poncho never adequately protecting oneself as the foxhole fills with water during monsoon season, the inability to ever have restorative sleep, the insatiable ever present hunger, the endless guard duty, not receiving mail from home, the existential chores of keeping an M16 or other weapon dry and cleaned, the boredom or the chaos of battle, the constant insatiable thirst or the desire and pristine thought-dream simply to drink a few swallows of the hot foul tasting canteen water during a fire fight?

Survival demanded focus every second of every day, every week, and every month until it was over.

How does one cradle in his arms a dying best friend, while shedding manly tears and creating that heart, broken for a lifetime of future and living with a hole in one's heart?

I do not believe I could bear it. Never in my life can I really 'know' what Grunts went through daily "outside the wire" during one's tour.

Just such a Grunt who served with distinction and extraordinary valor, compassion and a gifted talent for his quiet presence and gentle kindness with a heartfelt nonchalant promise that easily rolled off the tongue in the solemn promise of "I've got your back". This reciprocated trust created and established a palpable bond of brotherhood. Despite this fact any and every soldier suffered a certain dis-ease employing the ambitious and oft times illogical strategy of military policy in warfare gone amuck amidst the fog of war. Learning by doing and effectually mastering the application of rules throughout the entire Vietnam tour demanded cooperation, unique in all individual soldiers, to gain the essential necessary knowledge about the art and science of warfare and survival.

My husband Roger, also a disabled RVN Vet, and I had the honor of meeting Fr. Phil Salois during our first annual Vietnam Veteran Ministers' Conference more than twenty years ago. Father and several equally courageous RVN Veteran Ministers founded the Vietnam Veteran Ministers Conference years far gone and lost to the past. It has been well attended each year by old timers who were able to share their presence whenever possible and an ever-expanding circle of new faces, the newbies (FNG or Cherry) who didn't know what the week would bring, hesitant that they might remember too much and consequently 'lose it', and those of us suffering from the emotional pain and suffering of PTSD, known as the 'gift that keeps on giving'. There is a far more devastating additional cost to our identified Vietnam medical illnesses from our service, of which there are a myriad of complex, progressive and life-threatening maladies. It is perhaps the most damaging to the human soul: Spiritual Post Traumatic Disorder of the Spirit infected with the isolation and numbness that arises in the mind and costs all the treasure of our lives and that of our families, as they too suffer exquisitely the secondary passive smoke, pain and suffering throughout their lives.

Fr Phil, now a long-term member of the Catholic Order of La Salette Priests and his Merry Band of RVN Minister colleagues defined what Spiritual PTSD is for those of us who had never approached the problem of Spiritual Disorder in a specific and novel problem-solving, non-judgmental accepting methodology. They offered unique membership within the RVN Veteran Band of Brothers and selflessly shared their wisdom gleamed from countless meetings each year of the core group of founding members who 'walked the walk and talked the talk' of healing Spiritual Peace, that for so long, over decades has eluded and drained us of our core being and substance. This resulted in unknown damage and destruction to our family members, children, and beloved friends.

How did they accomplish this wonderous deed and goal-oriented journey of inner strength, wisdom, self-reflection and prayer, permitting specifically discovered knowledge throughout the journey of understanding what and why we are suffering, and how to bring about lost Spiritual Pain and suffering with Spiritual Peace via personal search within each distinctive person? Through various self-directed readings shared by and with other brother and sister Veterans who suffered with a distinctly identified Spiritual Deficit Disorder. Some veterans within our own group are published authors and practitioners of specific ministerial duties among both the veteran and civilian populations. The group membership has increased over the years with an expanding presence of guest academicians, repeaters and new attendees.

As an attending participant of multiple Conferences, I have developed an endearing relationship with Conference staff, in particular Fr. Phil Salois, Pastor Allen Cutter, Dr. Jonathan (Jack) Day and their wives who have shared much of themselves and have given thoughtful well-reasoned writings to Conference attendees in sessions exploring numerous topics relative to specific issues of Vietnam Veterans and a bazillion RVN Veterans, civilian guests and interested participants. We are blessed by Fr Phil's creativity and talents as a superb teacher and dearly loved friend whom we have known over the years.

These conferences given in November have become for me an annual marker in life spanning time since RVN service. We had previously lived in Media, Pennsylvania for twenty-five years raising our family of six children and caring for my parents. When each Fall arrived in all its spectacular colorful changes of seasons, and the Canadian geese could be heard as they made their trek south, I knew our Conference was rapidly approaching, particularly after the ancient Gingko tree dropped its leaves in one impressive night of the first chill and presented an excellent opportunity for introspection, reflection and evaluation of the year to decide where I was and where I was headed along my journey. The Conference posed an evaluation of time passing, what I had learned and what was out there yet to learn about Spiritual PTSD was shortly to be discovered. It became yet another gathering of eagles in our valuable lessons of healing comraderies and loving from these gifted Band of Brothers.

Regrettably, since Fr Phil and many other staff members were approaching retirement, the decision was made to end the formal Conferences in lieu of future independent informal meetings. I intensely miss our gatherings each Fall but have fond memories of our Conferences, content, attendees and the uniqueness of our Conference meetings.

Several years ago, we enjoyed the Conference Retreat Center invitation of a Military Chaplaincy who presented the incidence of Australian PTSD and Treatment methodology. It is fascinating to learn about military experience of PTSD and the varied treatments available to Veterans of international services.

Fr Phil invited Martin Webster, a UK soldier who served for many years in the British Army, proudly wearing the uniform of his Country.

Martin is a splendid UK combat veteran who Fr Phil attended the International Conference with in Palos Verdes, a Carmelite House located in Palos Verdes, California. Martin had multiple military deployments in Africa with the UN Forces and later during "The Troubles" and complexities of Northern Ireland. He also served in Iraq where he was exposed to constant imminent dangers of war and combat trauma. Upon returning to the UK, he experienced severe PTSD that caused significant life-altering events within himself, reflected in distraught relations with his family, children, service mates and friends.

Martin dealt with PTSD within the UK National Health Care System that does not have a dedicated VA equivalent, thus leaving the combat veteran who suffers with PTSD little support and treatment options. However, he navigated the System and progressed through phases of treatment to become an author, student and instructor of New Leaf Program (NLP), then with the application of NLP training and the support of Veterans enrolled in studies and treatment with the aid of NLP skills and adjunctive modalities, he initiated self-treatment with admirable, impressive success and improvement in his overall health and wellbeing.

I was fortunate to have been invited to the UK for six weeks and took classes with twenty NLP students in Manchester, UK. Fr Phil secured arrangements for me to attend the program.

In the classes, I was able to undertake two levels of competency and completed certification.

During our stay, we were able to attend a private four-day treatment cycle in Lourdes, France. The stark differences in acute management of combat trauma differ markedly from the American model of medication and psychotherapy. In the UK, no medication is used. This particular treatment model relies on core principles of NLP and the intense bonding of the Band of Brothers, not recreating the acute PTSD incident, but as they describe it, as "One step above the trauma". There is no direct approach to the actual traumatic combat event. There is no immersion into the traumatic incident. Success was clearly visible in two UK soldiers in an acute state of mental impairment whose very physical appearance visibly was transformed while their acute symptoms were profoundly diminished. Further treatment will be given as required as maintenance care. I was duly impressed by this brief, intense treatment.

None of these Conferences would have occurred without the dynamic leadership and kindness of Fr Phil Salois. I would never have studied in the UK nor witnessed the Rapid Trauma exposure and observable transformation of two acutely ill combat veterans. He has dedicated himself for decades to the American Vietnam population in his service as Chief

Chaplain of the Boston, MA VA Medical Center. His contact with these special hospitalized and out-patient gentlemen and ladies are challenging, and it takes a particularly well-trained and an efficient multifaceted team approach of specialized medical and extended multiple professionals to interact successfully with both the senior population as well as the young combat veteran who have recently served and demonstrate needs of acute care. The Chaplain is a strong addition to the team and serves as an integral contributing member of management of these two veteran populations: the elder who may well have been carrying around decades of untreated trauma or less than therapeutic treatment, and likewise, the young combat veteran who presents an acute need of immediate, appropriate care if it is to be successful and to restore health to a myriad of significant multiple horrific bodily injuries and disturbed psyche.

I would be remiss if I did not briefly discuss Fr Phil's supreme dedicated service to our splendid organization, Vietnam Veterans of America. He has willingly served as a Board Member and National Chaplain for many, many years and has had a remarkable and distinguished career filled with a lifetime of service to people, particularly those in need of his priestly ministrations.

The list of his accomplishments is endless and bespeaks his extraordinary life choices and journeys beginning as a young man, an Army soldier in Vietnam. That became for him a life-altering event influencing the course of service to his fellow man. Meritorious dedication to veteran patients, medical, nursing staff and ancillary staff personnel at the Boston VA Medical Center demonstrate this achievement over decades of service.

Having had a professional medical career for forty years, I am familiar with the critical demands and duties of hospital Chaplains. The tasks of a Chaplain are never finished because he must always be available at all hours of day or night for those patients in need of his support and Spiritual Ministrations.

Father is an amazing human being who serves his fellow men and women throughout the world.

He is the penultimate Man for All Seasons.

He is the penultimate Veteran for All Veterans.

Fr Phil Salois joins General MacArthur in the eternal Principles of Dedication, Commitment and Service.

Fr Phil, thank you, for being you. God bless and protect you always.

Kathleen Fennell
Army Nurse, Republic of Vietnam

I have many treasured memories of knowing and collaborating with Fr. Phil over the past two decades. I was first introduced to him by my dear friend Jonathan Shay, who urged me to get to know Fr. Phil. Jonathan spoke in glowing terms of Fr. Phil as a man devoted to the healing of spiritual wounds in war veterans. That first introduction led to many intermittent collaborations with Fr. Phil, who generously gave of himself to various projects and programs in Western Massachusetts, where I was based, and beyond. One of these was called Nostoi: Stories of War and Return, a series of forty lectures, workshops, film series, art projects, and community discussions, sponsored by Mass Humanities, the Veterans Education Project, the Five Colleges, and numerous other organizations, whose common aim was to sponsor dialogue and understanding between veterans and their communities. I recall too how Fr. Phil, Jonathan Shay, and I traveled to the Riverside Church in New York to serve as Commissioners at the "1st National Truth Commission on Conscience in War." Fr. Phil brought to this unique and crucial conclave not only pastoral wisdom and compassion as a priest ministering to the spiritually wounded, but also his own intense, distinguished, life-altering combat experience in Vietnam. I have learned so much from Fr. Phil over these years. One of the most important lessons I learned early from him was that combatants around the world in countless diverse conflicts suffer from much the same trauma and moral injury. The truth of this was confirmed for me since then as I came to know and work with combatants on every side in the Northern Irish Troubles, the South African border wars and internal anti-Apartheid conflicts, and now the war in Ukraine. Fr. Phil is, of course, most closely identified with the Vietnam War and with U.S. combat veterans; but equally impressive, I believe, is the extent of his work with veterans internationally across multiple continents. Another lesser-known accomplishment of Fr. Phil was his founding of an organization focused on the often unrecognized and unaddressed trauma suffered by military chaplains. My own collaborations and friendship with military chaplains have confirmed for me how crucial is this need to which Fr. Phil has pointed and given himself. In short, like so many others, I owe a profound debt of gratitude to Fr. Phil. He has kept his wartime promise to dedicate his life to veterans like himself and leaves behind a legacy of lifetime service.

Robert Emmet Meagher
Author of *Killing from the Inside Out* and
Herakles Gone Mad: Rethinking in an Age of Endless War

I met Phil at the first retreat that he organized for people who were both clergy and Vietnam Veterans. I had heard about it when he announced one Veterans Day, while making remarks at the Wall, that he was organizing such a group and to contact him. I think he recognized that being a veteran made a person a little bit strange, and being clergy did the same. And being both together really set one apart, and we needed to meet with others like ourselves.

The military experience is different from the civilian experience when it comes to religion. In the military, everyone is together. We respect religious differences, but don't let them divide us. I was a chaplain in Vietnam and really experienced that, but Phil, who was infantry and became a priest later, had the same sense. So, we got together, from Catholic to Assemblies of God and everyone in between, and we were bound together by the military experience and our faith involvement, but the differences didn't get in our way. And that characterized Phil. He was a priest, but he was a priest for everyone. And he loves being a Catholic priest, but doesn't let that get in the way.

Phil's major war story is his experience of being ambushed in Vietnam, and somehow, turnabout being fair play, engineering healing ambushes became part of his ministry. I will always give credit to Phil for saving my life emotionally. When I came back from Vietnam, I carried a lot of tears I could not express. I felt burned out in ministry and entered an alternate career of health care project management which didn't need to engage my emotions. My particulars may have been unique, but overall, it was a situation Phil encountered again and again, and his ministry to veterans was about healing those wounds. It wasn't at our first, but maybe the second annual meeting of our clergy veterans' group that he set up a healing service for veterans. It was an ambush. He pulled out all the stops. The scriptures were about the pain of coming home. The music was popular song after popular song that all spoke to coming home and not finding what one needed, what one hoped for. It got to me. I ended up crying for over half an hour, tears I had been carrying for decades.

After that, my life certainly contained the challenges everyone experiences, but living it was like moving from black and white to color. I will always be grateful to Phil for that.

Reverend Jackson H. Day
Retired Clergy, Baltimore-Washington Conference
United Methodist Church

This is an outstanding tribute to a wonderful priest of our Catholic faith. Fr. Phil has been the state chaplain of the Massachusetts American Legion for many, many years. He has been dedicated to the veteran members of our organization in his constant expression of Goodwill for God and Country. He has received a Silver Star for his heroic deeds in Vietnam.

We of the American Legion, the largest veterans' organization in the United States, appreciate hearing of his military exploits, with many of his fellow soldiers dying all around him in combat, and Fr. Phil promising the Good Lord that, if He allows him to return home unscathed, he would join him as a Catholic priest. And he did so, after informing his wonderful mother, even though he was an only child.

We on the national leadership of the American Legion were most proud to nominate and elect Fr. Phil as our National Chaplain, and he has done us proud, serving with distinction. Fr. Phil also serves as National Chaplain of the Vietnam Veterans of America and other veterans' organizations. He is dedicated and committed to giving back to his beloved country, which he served so well!

John P. "Jake" Comer
Past National Commander
American Legion

From reading the book thus far, you have learned what a remarkable man Phil is. His successes in the Veteran Community are common knowledge. He is a Combat Veteran of the Vietnam War and Silver Star Recipient. He became ordained after his Vietnam Service, where he was a "grunt" in the Army with a grenade launcher. He has served as National Chaplain for Vietnam Veterans of America for 30+ years, and the list of his accomplishments in the Veteran Community goes on and on. I have been fortunate enough to know this man as a Friend, Confidant, Counselor, Spiritual Advisor, and an Employer. I would like to share with you a few of my favorite stories about Phil, my Friend.

I remember the night my husband, John, came home from the meeting of the newly formed Vets group he and two friends, Joe Clougherty and Peter Caldarone, were trying to form. They had moved it from our living room to the upstairs meeting room in one of the social clubs in town for the first meeting of the Greater Attleboro Vietnam Veterans Association. I asked how the meeting went and he said, "It went well.

There was even a Priest from LaSalette who showed up, but he definitely isn't your typical priest – this guy is a riot."

A week or so later, this infant organization held its first fundraising event, a dance at the Attleboro Elks.

This was the typical start up deal – door charge, a deejay, and raffles. Phil spotted John and three of the other guys sitting at a table with their wives. He walked up to the table, stole a chair from another table and sat down between John and me. The wives were introduced, he talked a few more minutes, and then he asked me if I wanted to dance. Since John would rather eat glass than dance, I replied, "Definitely." This was the beginning of a long friendship.

We found out we had a lot in common, but dancing sealed the deal. We were both music buffs of '60's music, liked stage plays, especially musicals, and a love of life that included a twisted sense of humor. Conversation came easily and it wasn't long before he became part of the family, coming for supper at least once a week and spending Saturday nights at the house with the three other couples whom John and I were friendly. This is when the "Remember The Time When Phil…" stories started.

I remember when he asked me to take a ride to Plymouth with him to drop off Brochures at the Plymouth Travel Center for the upcoming LaSalette Festival of (Christmas) Lights. On the way home we ran out of gas on Route 95. Luckily just on the other side of the fence was the industrial park. The plan was that we would hop the fence and get my husband to bring us gas. He said he would hop it first so he could help me over it. The only problem was that while he was hopping the fence, he ripped the whole seat out of his black trousers. I was laughing so hard that I couldn't stand up straight and it started to downpour. I asked him to step back and made it over the fence on my own. We went into one of the businesses and successfully called John to come rescue us.

When our kids were about eight and ten years old, we replaced our beat-up living room set with a new sofa and a love seat. Phil came to supper two days later, got into a wrestling match with our son who was ten years old. While they were knocking each other around in the living room they both landed on the sofa. I heard a strange noise and found a spring sticking out the back of the brand-new sofa.

In the Spring of 1990, Phil announced at one of the GAVVA meetings that LaSalette had agreed to his proposal to start a ministry for Vietnam Veterans and their families. He described his vision for this organization, announced that LaSalette had offered him office space in the Provincial House, and that I would be running the office. This came as a total shock to me because he had forgotten to ask me about taking the job. I assured him several times that I would NOT be taking the job, he assured me that I was taking it, and in the summer of 1990, I went to work for him in a job that I held for 14 years.

He managed to talk John and I into hosting four Russians who were representing an international program for public libraries. They would be speaking in several cities in the United States, one of which was Attleboro. Phil thought it would be great fun if the four wives in the group cooked them a traditional Thanksgiving dinner. The Russians brought bottles of vodka and they all wound up getting buzzed. They had a speaking engagement at the Attleboro Library and we couldn't get them to leave. We finally sent them out with a homemade pie that they could eat at the hotel after they kept their engagement with the city.

The National Conference of Viet Nam Veteran Ministers played a big part in the dedication of the Women of the Vietnam War Memorial. There were week-long events which took place, one of which was a Women's Panel Discussion, which were made up of women veterans, and women who had been touched by the war other than as Veterans. I did not serve, but my husband did and I was asked to speak about how the war affected our children and myself. I hate public speaking, and I don't like being the center of attention. I was so nervous about this that I decided that morning before leaving I would read through my notes so I would be a bit calmer after a practice run. The only problem with this was that my counselor was on the other side of the adjoining bathroom door. She came in and flopped on the bed for an impromptu counseling session. When we left the Retreat House where we were staying, I listened intently to the other speakers and tried not to notice the people or the cameras. I was next to the last. When Phil introduced me as the wife of a Vietnam Veteran, I reached for my notes, only to find that I had left them on the table of my room and was going to have to do this without a net. I stepped up to the podium, introduced myself and gripped the sides of it tightly, and began to speak. I felt like I was going to be sick and pass out when Phil leaned over and whispered in my ear to "let go of the damned podium. You are shaking so bad that it sounds like machine gun fire coming through the mic and you're freaking out the vets." Surprisingly, that calmed me and I got through it without humiliating myself before the cameras.

So, there you have it. Some of my favorite "Phil My Friend" stories. He is truly one in a million.

Debbi McCallops
Former secretary for 14 years

I met Phil, who I would later call Father Brother Phil, in the early 90s at the PTSD clinic at the Providence VA Medical Center. He was easy to talk to and genuinely cared. He was a combat veteran and I felt comfortable with him. I had a fairly happy twenty years after returning from Vietnam, and then in 1989 I had a major meltdown and profound PTSD.

Our sessions were helpful and, as we built a friendship, he asked me to join him and read some of the things I wrote as a catharsis at what I affectionately called the Father Phil traveling Healing Show. We did a lot of that in different places and it was rewarding, although very difficult to share private things that I kept inside for years. At each one, it became easier to relate my pain and difficulties, especially seeing that it was helping others, which is what Phil did with everyone.

One of the greatest things Phil did for me was to find the parents of my dear friend and brother Stan, the death of him in Vietnam being my biggest loss and the most difficult to work through. I wrote to them and Stan's dad wrote back in one week and we continued our relationship until he passed on, and then Stan's mom wrote me. It was one of the most healing things I did for myself and for Stan's parents. I was like a son, and although never a replacement for Stan, it healed them because Stan was my best friend.

Over the years, Phil was/is one of the greatest assets in my recovery and healing. His compassion and empathy are of the highest caliber, and our friendship grew and will always be one of the blessings in my life. I am so pleased that I had my personal time with Phil, and that he is in my life. He will always have a special place in my heart.

With Phil's help and help from others, I am and have been for some time having a good life again and enjoying a high degree of recovery and happiness. Phil is an amazing man who is tireless in his journey to help others after Vietnam. He is a hero of mine and a friend and brother.

Bless the soul of Phil.

Ron Whitcomb
Vietnam combat vet, 1968-1969
Company C, 2/39th, 9th Infantry Division

My most fond memories of Fr. Phil were when he would bring important guests to VA Boston who knew who he was and valued his many accomplishments, first as a soldier, and then as a Catholic priest. Routinely, he would walk into my office with someone from California, Chicago, New York, all of whom were hoping to benefit from his wisdom and benevolence. Pretty soon, the visitors came from all parts of the world. His introduction of people to me was a true high point in my career, as I'd met most of the scientists in the world who studied psychological trauma, but Fr. Phil's contacts represented all types of people with the common bond that they experienced or helped people suffering the aftereffects of psychological trauma. As a combat veteran with a remarkable story of his time in the Vietnam war zone, Father Phil's story captivated all who listened to him.

Early on in our relationship, I invited him to speak with the members of the National Center for PTSD, which I direct. He was truly awe inspiring that morning as he described his war experiences and the point at which he vowed to dedicate his life to God. Of all the researchers, few of the members had themselves been to a war zone. My colleagues in the National Center, Dan and Lynda King (both psychological scientists), were deeply touched by Fr. Phil's experiences. Dan was seriously wounded in Vietnam and left blind, while Lynda was Dan's nursing student in Walter Reed Hospital. Fr. Phil became nothing short of a rock star in our VA Medical Center. Over time, all came to know and to deeply love him for his kind and gentle way with combat veterans with PTSD. He was a major asset to the National Center for PTSD, VA Boston Healthcare System, and the entire Veterans Health Administration. Observing this impressed upon me the need to understand on a first-hand basis the challenges felt by those touched by war.

Fr. Phil asked me on a few occasions to provide updates on the scientific knowledge accruing on PTSD and especially PTSD among Vietnam war veterans. I gladly traveled to whatever venue to present my knowledge derived from the scientific method. For me, it was a joy to watch him interact and interface with other war veterans, others who were clergy, and those affected by wars. Perhaps most profound was my gaining a more complete understanding of other ways of 'knowing', accumulating knowledge from other epistemological approaches. Likely, this was Fr. Phil's greatest gift to me, though I was a psychological scientist with a great interest in affecting public policy as it pertained to trauma. While my perspective was forged from data and science, Fr. Phil's came from humanism, philosophy, and theology; a powerful bond. Both are essential elements of a truly fine tapestry of our human existence. Knowledge stems from a synthesis borne of breadth to depth and then onto perspective. This was Fr. Phil's gift to me.

Terence M. Keane, PhD
Associate Chief of Staff for Research
VA Boston Healthcare System
Director: Behavioral Science Division
National Center for Posttraumatic Stress Disorder
Professor of Psychiatry & Assistant Dean for Research

I have been privileged to know "Father Phil" for over three decades. He is a man of great faith, courage and dedication. He is a soldier with combat experience and was awarded the Silver Star for gallantry in Vietnam. He is a man dedicated to serve our Lord Jesus Christ and minister to all of us with the same dedication and self-sacrifice as he served in the military. He is a superb example for all Americans and for Vietnam Veterans in particular.

As the Chaplain for Vietnam Veterans for decades, he is an example and inspiration for all of us. As a Christian, the experience of being around Fr. Phil is a reinforcement for my faith and belief that God is in control and will sustain us through life's journey. Veterans and others receive assurances from him as we face physical and psychological issues and the courage to live and excel. Prayer and the belief in God's power exude from every contact with this man of faith. I was the beneficiary of his ministry and compassion as I endured PTSD and recovered from leukemia associated with my Vietnam service.

I have served with Fr. Phil in the leadership of VVA and rely on his acceptance of my frailties, which allows me to approach him regardless of any circumstances. We share an eternal bond as Christian brothers that prevails over the worldly differences between us. Fr. Phil personifies all Jesus taught us about love and service to others. He works tirelessly to publish tributes to our Vietnam Veterans who have died, with no expectation of recognition, and he works to assure each individual is recognized with dignity and love.

Father Phil has had an immeasurable impact on my life by the way he lives, and I truly love him. He is always available and I keep his phone number and email address close by. The smile on the photograph on the cover of this book is emblematic of his life. God bless you my special friend, Father Philip Salois.

Dr. Wayne Reynolds, PhD
Vietnam Veterans of America-National Treasurer

I was sitting in the backyard of the Brown ancestral home, having nearly finished my first year in the seminary. My whole family was there; we had just completed my mother's funeral. We had gathered like this just six months earlier, after burying my dad. I was devastated. As a sign of love and support, many La Salette priests and brothers were there, among them the vocation director. I never learned why, but accompanying him was a young man interested in our community. The man came over and introduced himself as Phil Salois. I don't remember what he said as he offered his condolences, but I do remember thinking, "I hope he joins us; I think we could be friends." He did join us, and a year and a half later, we were living together in Cambridge, Massachusetts, studying at the Weston Jesuit School of Theology.

We did become friends. In the year and a half that we had together, I learned that Phil was warm, compassionate, funny, and loving. Living with Phil was like living in a musical. He had a song for everything. I knew he was a veteran, had been in Vietnam, but never really heard his story. He didn't speak a lot about his 'war' days. One evening at our weekly community meeting, Phil opened up, and he finally broke his silence. He told us of his days in Vietnam and his dramatic rescue of other Army buddies. He was not only my friend but also someone I admired. I was glad he didn't have to carry that burden by himself anymore.

I was ordained, and a few years later Phil was ordained as well. When he was given permission to start the Ministry to Vietnam War Veterans, I thought, "This is where this man belongs." I had experienced his kind, compassionate heart, and now it would be given to people who needed the healing love. He could reach out with authority to these vets because he had been there. Phil always ministers from a place of integrity, and I think his fellow vets knew they were talking with 'a brother' who knew their lives. I have always felt blessed to call Phil a friend. He offered support from day one, and now, 45 years later, we still try to support each other.

Father Edward "Ted" Brown, M.S.
Missionary of Our Lady of La Salette
Director of the Center of Christian Living
Attleboro, Massachusetts

I remember being at Triple D's with Fr. Phil and our friend Marie and we asked him how he came to be a priest. He vividly described his experience in Vietnam in a foxhole. He talked about bullets flying and bodies dropping and having to drag them into the hole. He said, "God, please, if you get me out of here, I'll serve you forever."

Fr. Phil was the first priest that I worked with at the VA who was a Veteran. His interactions with our Veterans were different than I'd seen with other priests. I believe that the shared experiences were the reasons, brother to brother, a true bond that is special and only understood by those who have lived through the same challenges.

Joan Clifford DNP, RN, FACHE, NEA-BC
Medical Center Director
Edith Nourse Rogers Memorial Veterans Hospital
Bedford, Massachusetts

I joined VVA in 1987. Now, at the age of 76, the timeline of my history with the Vietnam Veterans of America becomes somewhat of a blur. But it's a long story in the making and one I will never forget or regret. It changed forever the direction of my life on many fronts. It was after attending my first National VVA convention in 1989 that I was thrust into the world of the veteran activist role, most particularly on the federal level within the organization.

It was in this arena that I met and came to know Father Phil Salois. No longer do I remember exactly when our introduction took place. I believe it was in the late 1990's, but like so many somewhat casual unremarkable events and meetings, they just *were*. It was my good fortune, maybe destiny, that our acquaintance developed into a friendship and him as a counselor.

The world of the Veteran Community is one of tight exclusivity in many respects...protective of its own. And so, it was in our world of Veteran camaraderie, Phil, as we sometimes called him, was a likeable guy (some might say a character) who shared jokes and stories that entertained us all. But he had the profound and uncanny ability to turn around, step back and attend to the needs of both the struggling individual before him and the group in front of him. He understood empathy. He was a scholar of PTSD and as such he *knew* us...*He got us*.

He could have a soft quiet approach when heartfelt conversation was most needed...he had the right words to calm the soul, to lend his gift of understanding when a heart was in pain and most in need, a solid, firm strength when one was seeking direction or solace. And then again, he could also be a jokester...an impish little guy in the blink of an eye and a quick wink. I think he truly embraced this side of his personality.

We trusted his counsel in which he was never judgmental. He was a true gift and a treasure to so many souls.

He also recognized truth from BS.

Over all the years he served our VVA community of Veterans and their families he continued to be extremely active in our organizational events in Washington, and across the country. He was present and offered Holy Mass at the National Cathedral of the Immaculate Conception upon the approval of a most significant recognition of the contribution of women who served in the military during the Vietnam Era...the Vietnam Women's Memorial located directly across from The Vietnam Veterans Wall.

Fr. Phil kept us sadly aware of the passing of our fellow VVA members by establishing a column in our National VVA Magazine providing information on our fallen friends. He served on several National VVA Committees, providing grief counseling, fostered PTSD awareness and helped many of us face our fears...helping us face the truth in our lives, the blessings we were given, comfort for our pain, and disappointments, prepared always to quietly sit with us and just *be*.

His life was one of dedicated service, helping his fellow Veterans survive in the world without and within.

He served his promise well. And Mary smiled!

Martha Four, RN
Vietnam Veteran Nurse, 1969-1970
18th Surgical Hospital, Quang Tri, Vietnam (near the DMZ)
Bronze Star Recipient
Past National Vice-President, Vietnam Veterans of America

"As a State Representative, you will meet people that you wouldn't have come into contact with otherwise, and you will make friendships that will last a lifetime." Those were my father's words to me back in 2006 when I was first elected to the Rhode Island House of Representatives. When I met Father Philip Salois for the first time, my father's prophetic words could not have been more accurate. I may never have met Father Phil otherwise, and I have been grateful ever since.

When I first heard Father Phil give the invocation at an event held by the United Veterans Council of Woonsocket, I was instantly moved and at peace.

His gentle manner of speaking, his loving prayers, and his true love for veterans and all they have given shone through immediately. As time went by, I found myself looking forward to these events, if only to hear the prayerful words of my friend.

It was only years later when I would come to learn that the gentle, thoughtful, and inspirational man that I had befriended was, in a past life, a hero and a warrior. Father Phil never speaks about the past, always remaining the humble servant of the Lord. You'll never find him looking for accolades, but rather trying to find ways to bring comfort and peace to the lives of our Nation's veterans. As I learned more about the bravery and heroics of Father Phil, it finally dawned on me why the Lord granted him the courage and strength on the battlefield that fateful day. The Lord had a plan for Philip Salois, he was destined to be the savior of men, both on the battlefield, and in their souls.

Jon Brien, Attorney at law
Rhode Island House of Representatives
District #49-Woonsocket, North Smithfield

I have been friends with Fr. Philip Salois for many years, since the early days of the Vietnam Veterans of America (VVA). I always thought that he was an exceptional candidate to serve as chaplain for a veteran's organization. His service as a soldier before becoming a priest, combined with his heroism as denoted by his being awarded a Silver Star, gave him credibility that enabled him to get close with the veterans he served in the VA system for so many years. This credibility was further enhanced by his bubbly personality and kindness. I am proud to call Fr. Phil a friend.

John Rowan
President & CEO, 2005-2021
Vietnam Veterans of America

Phil and I served in the same company in Vietnam but in different platoons. On March 1, 1970, Phil's platoon was walking in front of my platoon when we walked into a well-organized U-shaped ambush that lasted many hours. We suffered 2 Killed in Action and many Wounded in Action that day. Phil left his position to help his buddies who were pinned down by the enemy and separated from our columns. We really didn't know one another then because we were in different platoons.

In 2000, my company started having reunions thanks mostly to Phil and other members of his platoon. Through these gatherings, I have gotten reunited with Vietnam buddies and have been able to get past some of the emotional issues the war has caused me. Phil will always be a hero to me both on and off the battlefield for that reason. Father Phil has become a very good friend of mine. He has spent his entire priesthood helping veterans recover from the effects of war. I am proud to call him my Brother!

Jersey Joe Washart
1st Platoon

Fr. Philip Salois, "Phil", a man I am proud and honored to call my friend. As a nurse working at the BVAMC with many Vietnam veterans, I came to know Phil and quickly learned about his mission to work with our Vietnam vets. Fr. Phil's combat experience made him credible and relatable with Vietnam vets, and he was able to earn their trust. Many of these vets, who were shut down for years, sought forgiveness and were able to begin their journey of healing that some psychiatrists were unable to "treat" with medications or counseling.

Fr. Phil was ever visible and interactive with all our veterans and with staff. His compassion and great sense of humor were evident in these relationships. I often think, just as Jesus was a man of his times, so was and is Fr. Phil! I am so looking forward to reading Phil's life story; it's truly a life story that deserves to be shared with ALL people. Now, I'm just wondering who's going to play the role of Philip Salois in the film!

Congratulations, Phil, your story deserves to be heard!

Geri McCabe, RNC, BSN
Head Nurse, Psychiatry-Retired
Jamaica Plain (Boston) VA Medical Center

CHAPTER 16

One Man's Impact on The World

"I was in a very dark place and meeting Philip changed my life in so many ways. Sharing stories with Vietnam veterans helped me forgive myself and restore my faith in life and humanity. Philip's work over decades since the Vietnam War has saved thousands of lives from the ripple effect of the men and women he has shown his love to."

Martin Webster, Truro, United Kingdom

I am a former British Army Veteran of three conflicts, Iraq, Northern Ireland and Sierra Leone. I was diagnosed with PTSD in 2007 after twelve years of service as a Corporal.

Father Phil reached out to me in 2010 and invited me to his spiritual retreat in 2011 in Florida. I was in a very dark place and meeting Philip changed my life in so many ways. Sharing stories with Vietnam veterans helped me forgive myself and restore my faith in life and humanity. Philip's work over decades since the Vietnam War has saved thousands of lives from the ripple effect of the men and women he has shown his love to. I'm blessed to have been at five of the retreats, and what they have done for so many veterans and their families is a modern-day achievement. He has given so much to so many people and changed the lives of veterans forever. I will never forget the stories and the lifelong friends I've bonded with over those retreats, and they quite possibly saved my life in some of my darkest days. After Philip's help, I went on to set up my unit helping veterans with PTSD in the UK and made two films on Amazon Prime called *Diary of a Disgraced Soldier* and *The Penitent*. I owe a lot of the story in those films to working with Philip and I hope one day to bring his story to the big screen. He is a special soul who will hate this praise of his work, as he sees it as his calling. I'm sure that Private Klug, who he left behind, and his platoon commander in Vietnam will be immensely proud of what this remarkable Private soldier has accomplished in all these years since that horrific bloodbath that killed so many people.

There are many Priests in the world doing good deeds, but this Priest has gone beyond the call of duty and has earned his wings.

It was emotional writing this as he is loved by so many. Philip Salois is the real deal.

Martin Webster
Truro, United Kingdom

I had the great fortune to meet Father Phil in 2003 at a spiritual healing retreat in the U.S.A. At the time, I had just returned from a six-month deployment on a Canadian warship in the Arabian Sea supporting an American Naval Task Force hunting for AlQaeda operatives. It was the summer of 2002. I was the senior chaplain for the three- ship Canadian complement to the American operation.

After my deployment, I began to research protocols for healing the spiritual wounds of military service personnel. I came across Father Phil's Vietnam Veteran Ministers' organization and noted their work in this space. I was delighted when the organization became international in scope and I became a member along with an Anglican priest from the U.K., who was a former British Army officer who later became a Royal Marine Chaplain. We actually happened to be in the Middle East at the same time in 2010.

My membership in the group was transformational. Since my return to the USA after serving in Beirut as a US Marine Guard in the early 1980s, I longed to meet a priest who had been in combat, so that I could have the opportunity to share my Beirut experience and come to terms on a spiritual level with what I had experienced during my 12-month tour there in the middle of Lebanon's Civil War. Father Phil was that priest. Carrying the wounds of war is a very lonely experience. The protocol that Father Phil and his magnificent colleagues in the group he founded remains a ground-breaking and vital ministry for all active-duty military personnel and veterans who grapple spiritually with the trauma of war.

I became a Canadian Chaplain because I married a Canadian and immigrated to Canada. My wife and I are now retired from military chaplaincy, having transferred in the Australian Defense Force where we served as military chaplains. We now continue our ministry helping those who have suffered Church abuse here in Australia using Fr. Phil's legacy as part of our inspiration.

Father Phil is not only a bona fide military hero, he is among the grouping of truly wonderful priests Jean and I have had the blessing to know in the world.

Joseph F. Johns
Chaplain (Squadron Leader)
RAAF Retired
Clare Valley, Australia

Father Philip... What can I tell you about this man... about this personality...?

I met Father Philip back in 1998. I then worked in the union of veterans (NGO).

At that time, our country, Georgia, was going through hard times, the devastation after the war and the occupation by Russia of 20% of the territory of Georgia and other delights of the post-Soviet and post-war period.

During this aforementioned period, we had an idea to organize in Georgia, in Tbilisi, an international conference of veterans "Peaceful Caucasus". I sent an email with an offer to participate in the above conference to the Vietnam Veterans of America (VVA). I received an answer to my email from Father Philip, and from that moment on, we started a real friendship.

It can be said that we have become in some sense - "Brothers in Arms", despite the fact that both of us soldiers defended the interests of different countries in the past. Father Philip defended the interests of the Democratic camp, and I unfortunately defended the interests of the Communist regime.

I found in this man not only a true friend, but also an interesting versatile personality, with a kind and magical character. His charisma and determination conquered me.

Father Philip took an active part in organizing our conference.

Thanks to him, in the difficult post-war period, (the first war with Russia in Abkhazia in 1992-1993) representatives of several countries came to Georgia.

Father Philip was the first to arrive in Tbilisi and, together with me, met all the guests at the airport.

There were interesting discussions and meetings; the conference was a success thanks to the active participation of Father Philip.

It was at that time the biggest success of Georgia in the international arena.

This man combines the courage of a fighter and the tact of a priest at the same time.

I can probably talk about this person endlessly, since it is impossible to say everything about him. I am grateful to him for his friendship with me.

Michael Tsikaridze
Georgian Veterans Federation

Fr. Phil Salois-what a legend; a wise, big-hearted, generous, gorgeous human being. An owl of a man. He contacted me many years ago in his role as Secretary to the International Conference of War Veteran (ICWVM) Ministers. Over some years, I received these beautiful envelopes from him in the mail, which often included air tickets to fly from Great Britain to attend a ICWVM retreat somewhere in the USA. Through his and ICWVM's generosity, I was able to attend a number of annual veterans' retreats where I first met Fr. Phil, Alan, Jack, and Linda. It was like meeting Moses, Joshua, Aaron, and 'Sister sarge' (no Old Testament character could match her!). I haven't seen him for a number of years, but I remember Fr. Phil being regal: majestic in insight. He could sniff out bullshit and inauthenticity, and then he would wave it away with a flick of the hand. He was also deeply compassionate, with a compassion that resonated through his being, radiating signals of genuine kindness, that brought reassurance. For me personally, I encountered in Fr. Phil, and the ICWVM team, a group of veterans who had seen some very significant 'action', not just militarily in Vietnam, but also in life. I felt safe enough to be open and honest about my own struggles as a British Army veteran, and the way they were impacting my own life and relationships. I felt safe enough to talk about trauma and brokenness. Fr. Phil embodied non-judgmental listening. I will always remember a session he led at the first retreat I attended in Attleboro, Massachusetts. We were invited 'to lay something down' within a sacred circle, like an emotion or an experience. I lay down my desire to kill. It was the start of a long process, but I will always be grateful to Fr. Phil for the invitation and opportunity to make a start. I am also grateful for this opportunity to write a few words about Fr. Phil. He is a brother of mine. He is like an older brother who put his arm around me, smiled, and showed by his example and intellect a different way. I remember him with love; a very small portion of the abundant love that he so deserves. Kindness and peace be always with him.

Reverend Andrew Rawding
Anglican Minister
Belfast, Ireland

It is important that your life's achievements be recaptured. We last saw each other some eighteen years ago at the International Vietnam Veterans Ministers Conference in Attleboro, Massachusetts in 2005. God's richest blessings on you and all the brothers and sisters. Much love to you all. Grace and Peace from Down Under.

Rev. Wally Te Ua
Anglican priest
Vietnam Veteran
2nd Royal Australian Regiment/New Zealand
Gisborne, New Zealand

Conclusion

In addition to being our nation's longest conflict, the war in Vietnam was also one of America's deadliest.[81] With 58,220 casualties, Vietnam ranks behind only the two World Wars and the Civil War in terms of the number of American deaths. Cemeteries here and abroad mark the graves of hundreds of thousands who have made the ultimate sacrifice in the service to their country. All of those who gave the last full measure should be considered heroes, for they certainly are. War has also produced many other shining stars. Their stories may never be told, and some stories may never be known, but they are heroes still.

Very few people voluntarily leave home and family to go to a foreign war-torn country where survival becomes the only way of life. No one longs to spend countless days and nights in the muddy trenches of a booby-trapped, ant, mosquito and snake-infested jungle knowing the very next step could be the last. And no one wants to risk capture where the threat of constant physical, mental and psychological torture can make each day seem like a never-ending nightmare with death marking your only relief. That is the story of the Vietnam War, but the story doesn't end there and neither did the suffering.

Perhaps the cruelest part of the war for those returning to the states was the abandonment by the very people for whom the soldiers spent endless days fighting. Many returned to face a new world of loneliness, fear and anxiety. Suffering from diagnosed or undiagnosed post-traumatic stress disorder, many veterans were triggered by sights, sounds and smells that caused them to return, mentally at least, to those jungles where ruthless enemies sought to inflict as much physical and psycho-

---

[81] Wikipedia, United States Military Casualties of War, https://en.wikipedia.org/wiki/United_States_military_casualties_of_war.

logical pain as humanly possible. PTSD made it nearly impossible for many of those veterans to hold a job and many others were forced to face a future of homelessness or suicide as a result.

Twenty-one-year-old Philip Salois was seemingly just one more soldier fighting in Vietnam for a cause that he really didn't quite understand. When his platoon was unwittingly dispatched into a horseshoe-shaped Viet Cong ambush, several men in the forward unit became trapped under enemy fire. Despite orders from his commanding officer, Salois refused to leave those men behind, opting instead to rescue his fellow soldiers. With one other brave soul offering assistance, Salois belly-crawled into harm's way, not once, but three times, until all six men, or their lifeless bodies, were reunited with their companions. For his efforts, Salois was awarded the Silver Star for bravery. Salois' wartime heroics, however, were just beginning.

Keeping a promise he made to God during that bloody engagement, Salois became a priest who spent the next forty years fighting to protect those veterans whose return to the states was far less than they had hoped it might be. Fighting off his own PTSD demons, Fr. Phil, as he became known, organized reunions, retreats, and veteran support groups. He helped countless veterans of foreign wars, and their spouses, deal with the emotional and psychological traumas that prevented them from enjoying the fullness of life. In short, like the twenty-one-year-old boy in the jungles of Vietnam, Fr. Phil saved the lives of those soldiers in so many ways.

Some heroes are made on the battlefield while others are made during the throes of everyday life by making the extraordinary seem ordinary. Fr. Phil was certainly a hero in the jungles of Vietnam, but his true heroism surfaced in his humanitarian work right here in the streets of America.

Appendices

Appendix A
Service-Related Awards and Honors

Left: A selection of U.S.Army medals awarded to Fr. Phil. (Top row L-R) Silver Star Medal for Valor; Bronze Star for Meritorious Service; Air Medal. (Bottom row L-R) Army Commendation Medal with Two Oak Leaf Clusters; Good Conduct Medal; Vietnam Service Medal with Two Campaign Stars; National Defense Medal. (Shadow box of medals courtesy of Fr. Phil Salois. Photo taken by the author.)

Right: Fr. Phil (center) and his mom Hélène are all smiles following Fr. Phil's Silver Star Pinning Ceremony. Pictured with them is Major General Stones of the 94th ARCOM. (Photo courtesy of Fr. Phil Salois)

1. **Silver Star (The third highest medal given in the Armed Forces)**
   Citation, October 8, 1970:
   The President of the United States of America, authorized by Act of Congress July 9, 1918 (amended by act of July 25, 1963), takes pleasure in presenting the Silver Star to Specialist Fourth Class Philip Gaston Salois (ASN: 56737963), United States Army, for gallantry in action in connection with military operations involving conflict with an armed hostile force in the Republic of Vietnam. Specialist Fourth Class Salois distinguished himself by exceptionally valorous actions on 1 March 1970 while serving as a rifleman assigned to Company A, 3d Battalion,

7th Infantry Regiment, 199th Infantry Brigade. On this date, Specialist Salois was participating in a platoon size operation when his unit was engaged by a platoon of North Vietnamese Army regular soldiers. In the initial moments of contact five members of the platoon became separated from the main element and were in extreme danger of being overrun by the enemy. Specialist Salois and two other men immediately volunteered to attempt the rescue of the stranded element. As they reached two of the trapped men, intense enemy fire forced Specialist Salois and his two comrades back to the platoon perimeter. When another soldier tried again to reach the trapped element, he was mortally wounded. Without regard for his personal safety, Specialist Salois maneuvered through the intense enemy fire and retrieved the body of his mortally wounded comrade. Then for a third time, Specialist Salois and another man left the perimeter, reached the separated element, and successfully maneuvered the stranded element back to the perimeter. Specialist Salois' gallantry in action reflects great credit upon himself, his unit and the United States Army.

2. **Meritorious Service Medal**
The Meritorious Service Medal is a military award presented to members of the United States Armed Forces who distinguished themselves by outstanding meritorious achievement or service to the United States subsequent to January 16, 1969.

3. **Combat Infantryman's Badge**
The Combat Infantryman's Badge is a United States Army military decoration. The badge is awarded to infantrymen and Special Forces soldiers in the rank of colonel and below, who fought in active ground combat while assigned as members of either an Infantry or Special Forces unit brigade size or smaller at any time after December 6, 1941. Specifically, it recognizes the inherent sacrifices of all infantrymen, and that they face a greater risk of being wounded or killed in action than any other military occupational specialties.

4. **Vietnam Service Medal**
The Vietnam Service Medal is a military award of the United States Armed Forces established on July 8, 1965 by order of President Lyndon B. Johnson. The medal is awarded to recognize service during the Vietnam War by all members of the U.S. Armed Forces provided they meet the award requirements.

5. **Republic of Vietnam Campaign Medal**

The Republic of Vietnam Campaign medal is a South Vietnamese military campaign medal given to U.S. military personnel who contributed direct combat support to the Republic of Vietnam Armed Forces for at least six months.

6. **Air Medal**

During the Vietnam War, the U.S. Army awarded the Air Medal to infantry troops who flew on combat assault missions.

7. **Army Commendation Medal with three Oak Leaf Clusters**

The Army Commendation Medal is awarded to any member of the Armed Forces of the United States other than General Officers who, while serving in any capacity with the U.S. Army after December 6, 1941, distinguished themselves by an act of heroism, extraordinary achievement, or significant meritorious service which has been of mutual benefit to the friendly nation and the United States.

8. **Army Achievement Medal with two Oak Leaf Clusters**

The Army Achievement Medal acknowledges those in service who demonstrate outstanding achievement or meritorious service of military personnel in either combat or noncombat situations based on sustained performance or specific achievement of a superlative nature.

9. **Good Conduct Medal**

The Army Good Conduct Medal is given to any enlisted U.S. Army personnel who carry out at least one year of "honorable and faithful service" while the United States is at war.

10. **National Defense Service Medal**

The National Defense Service Medal is a service award of the United States Armed Forces established by President Dwight D. Eisenhower in 1953. It is awarded to every member of the U.S. Armed Forces who served during any one of four specified periods of armed conflict or national emergency from June 7, 1950 through December 31, 2022.

11. **DAV Distinguished VA Employee of the Year Medal.**

12. **Commissioned a 1st Lieutenant Priest-Chaplain in the United States Reserves (1990).**

Assigned to 455th Field Hospital, Providence, RI

13. **Assigned to 883rd Medical Company, Combat Stress Control**

Resigned Commission in 2002.

Appendix B
Clergy-Related Awards and Honors

Priestly duties are dedicated in service to war veterans with a specialty in the spiritual healing for those suffering from Post-Traumatic Stress Disorder (PTSD).

1. **Chief of Chaplain Service for the VA Boston Healthcare System**

2. **Chaplain at the VA New England Healthcare System**

3. **National Recipient of the Celtic Cross Award from the Catholic War Veterans**
   Fr. Salois opened a Catholic War Veterans Chapter in Attleboro, MA (PT 109 Chapter). For his efforts while acting on behalf of the chapter, he was rightly given national recognition with the Celtic Cross Award.

The Catholic War Veterans of the USA honored Fr. Phil with The Celtic Cross Award. (Award courtesy of Fr. Phil Salois. Photo taken by the author)

4. **Life Achievement for Outstanding Service to the Veteran Community from the Vietnamese-American Veterans of New England and Canada**

5. **Veterans' Affairs Chaplain of the Year by Military Chaplains Association**

6. **Chapter of Four Chaplains Humanitarian Award**
   Membership in the Legion of Honor of the Chapel of Four Chaplains is awarded based on documented acts of selfless service. Selfless service consists of deeds and actions on behalf of others irrespective of their race, ethnicity or faith.
   The Legion of Honor Humanitarian Award is given in recognition of a lifetime

A multitude of Vietnam Veteran organizations presented Fr. Phil with the 2000 Lifetime Achievement Award for Devotion, Integrity, Selflessness, High Principles and Hard Work in support of their cause. (Award courtesy of Fr. Phil Salois. Photo taken by the author)

commitment to selfless service and societal advancement that has demonstrably affected the quality of life in the individual's community or region.

The Chapel of Four Chaplains presented their 2001 Humanitarian Award and their 2002 Legion of Honor Bronze Medallion Award to Fr. Phil for his service to others regardless of faith. (Awards courtesy of Fr. Phil Salois. Photos taken by the author)

7. **Chapel of Four Chaplains Bronze Medallion Award**
   In the Four Chaplains Memorial Foundation, the Legion of Honor Bronze Medallion is the second highest award and is granted for extraordinary contributions to the well-being of others in the State, Regional or National Level.

8. **Knights of Columbus Lantern Award (2014)**

   The Lantern Award is an appropriate way to honor those who reflected the religious and patriotic ideals of the Founding Fathers. Named for the Lanterns placed in the tower of the Old North Church in Boston to warn Paul Revere, the award is given by the Massachusetts State Council and is presented at their Patriot's Day Dinner.

   Massachusetts State Council of the Knights of Columbus presented Fr. Phil with their highest honor, the Lantern Award, in 2014. (Award courtesy of Fr. Phil Salois. Photo taken by the author)

Appendix C
Memberships in Veterans Service and Historical Organizations

1. **The American Legion**
   Life member since 1987
   Massachusetts Post #20 and Massachusetts Department Chaplain since 1990
   Appointed National Chaplain in 2019

2. **Veterans of Foreign Wars.**
   Life member and Chaplain to Rhode Island Post #11519

3. **Disabled American Veterans**
   Life member and Chaplain to Rhode Island Chapter #12

4. **Vietnam Veterans of America**
   Life member
   National Chaplain since 1994
   President of James M. Ray Memorial Chapter #818 since 1975

5. **Military Order of Foreign Wars**
   National Chaplain since 2017
   Chaplain to the Rhode Island Commandery since 2016

6. **AMVETS**
   Life member

7. **Catholic War Veterans**
   Life Member

8. **World Veterans Federation**
   Presented work on PTSD at International Conference, Dubrovnik, Croatia (1998)

9. **Peace Caucusus Conference, Tbilisi, Georgia (1999)**
   Speech to veterans of USSR's war in Afghanistan

10. **Knights of Columbus**
    Member

11. **Military Chaplains Association**
    Member

12. **National Association of Veterans Affairs Chaplains**
    Member

13. **National Conference of Veterans Affairs Catholic Chaplains**
    Member

14. **Reserve Officers Association**
    Member

15. **American-French Genealogical Society**
    2014 inductee in the French-Canadian Hall of Fame for military service and for devotion to the military veterans.

16. **United States Veterans Council of Woonsocket, Rhode Island**
    2014 Veteran of the Year

17. **Anticipated Induction into the Rhode Island Heritage Hall of Fame.**
    Nominated by Board Member Albert Beauparlant in 2023.

Appendix D
Excerpt From the Agenda of the November 10, 1993
National Conference of Vietnam Ministers, Featuring One of the Women's Events

Wednesday, November 10, 1993
Morning Session: 9:00 A.M. to 12:30 P.M.
Women's Panel Discussion – Vista Hotel, Washington, DC

Theme: "Women of Faith/Women of Valor"- Phil Salois, Presiding

Focused on the Spiritual Healing of the Women of the Vietnam War. The Panel was expanded to include both women veterans and women civilians connected with the war.

Panel Participants:

Jessica Wolfe, Ph.D., Director of Women's health Sciences Division of the National Center for Post-Traumatic stress Disorder, Boston VAMC, Boston, Massachusetts.

Kathy Neil, M.S.W., a member of the Clinical Team of the Providence (R.I.) VA Medical Center's PCT (Post-Traumatic Stress Disorder Clinical Team) with special focus on Vietnam Veteran Wives and Significant Others Support Groups.

Jeanne Penfold, National president of American Gold Star Mothers, Incorporated, Washington, DC. Mother of Peter Penfold, KIA.

Rita Quimby of Cambridge, Massachusetts. Mother of an In-Country Vietnam Veteran Suffering from PTSD.

Nancy Kellar of Moody, Maine. Widow of Vietnam Air Force SGT. Stanley Yurewicz.

Maureen Dunn of Randolph, Massachusetts. POW Wife of CMDR. Joseph P. Dunn, U.S. Navy Aviator. Ms. Dunn serves on the Board of *National League of Families.*

Lynda Van Devanter-Buckley of Herndon, Virginia. Vietnam Veteran, U.S. Army Nurse, Author of *Home Before Morning* and contributor to *Visions of War, Dreams of Peace.*

Barbara Lilly of Bowie, Maryland. American Red Cross-Recreation Program (Mobile) Recreation Aide.

Cathleen Cordova of Pleasanton, California. Department of the Army Civilian with Special Services Army Service Club Director.

Sally Vinyard of Fallbrook, California. U.S. Navy-OICC and Defense Attache Office/Chief Housing officer, served 72 months in Vietnam and was involved in "Operation Baby Lift."

Laura Palmer of New York City, New York. Vietnam War Correspondent, journalist, author of *Shrapnel in the Heart, Come Here,* and *In the Absence of Angels.* Currently a producer with NBC News in New York.

Debbi McCallops of North Attleboro, Massachusetts. Vietnam Veteran Wife and Administrative Assistant to the NCVNVM.

Patience Mason of Gainesville, Florida. Vietnam Veteran Wife of author Bob Mason (*Chicken Hawk,* and *Return to chicken Hawk).* Patience is the author of *Recovering From The War.*

Le Ly Hayslip of San Francisco, California. Vietnamese woman. President and Founder of *East Meets West Foundation.* Author of *When Heaven and Earth Changed Places* and *Child of War, Woman of Peace.* Le Ly is the subject of the full-length feature film, *Heaven and Earth,* in Oliver Stone's Vietnam War film trilogy. She is the ex-wife of a U.S. Army G.I.

Ahn Ryan of Plymouth, Massachusetts. Vietnamese woman and Interpreter for the U.S. Army Intelligence and is the ex-wife of a U.S. Army G.I.

Noon: Luncheon, Vista Hotel-Honoring Women of the Vietnam War (Sponsored by Vietnam Veterans of America Women's Committee)

4:30 P.M. Eucharistic mass of Thanksgiving Honoring Women Veterans

Crypt Church of the Basilica, national Shrine of the Immaculate Conception

This special Mass was celebrated to honor Women Veterans as they prepared to dedicate the Vietnam Veteran Women's Memorial and to honor and recognize the service of the Civilian Women who served in Vietnam.

The Mass used was the Votive Mass of Our Lady of La Salette.

Individual portraits of the eight nurses who died in Vietnam were placed on easels, 4 on each side of the altar. A large red votive burned on the floor of each portrait. The portraits were supplied by Doreen Spelts.

Principal Celebrant for the Mass was His Excellency the Most Reverend Joseph T. Dimino, D.D., Archbishop for the Military Services, U.S.A.

Most Reverend Francis X. Roque, D.D., Most Reverend John G. Nolan, D.D., Most Reverend John J. Glynn, D.D., Auxiliary Bishops of the Military Archdiocese, Reverend Monsignor Roger

J. Brady, Department of Veterans Affairs National Director of the Chaplain Center, Reverend Richard J. Dunne, VA Region 1 Regional Chaplain, Reverend Richard Shannon, and Reverend Paul F. deLadurantaye, Director of Liturgy of the National Shrine of the Immaculate Conception concelebrated the Mass.

Reverend Philip G. Salois, M.S. was the homilist and Reverend Kenneth Herbster was the Master of Ceremonies.

Readings were proclaimed by Admiral Frances Buckley, U.S.N., Ret., and Major Linda Spoonster-Schwartz, U.S. Air Force, Retired, General Intercessions by Joan Furey, former Army Nurse, Vietnam.

Family members from 3 of the eight nurses' families were present for the Mass. A childhood friend represented another family. During the presentation of gifts, a floral spray made up of a lily and a red rose tied with a maroon ribbon was placed above the portraits of the nurses. A Book of Honor which lists the names of the 56 Civilian Women who lost their lives in Vietnam was placed on the altar during the offertory procession. This book was carried enthroned on the altar by a Civilian Woman who served in Vietnam.

Post communion Meditation *"A White Mass"* was delivered by Doreen Spelts, author of the book *"…there are eight of them."*

Special thanks go to:

Dr. Leo Cornelius Nestor, Director of Music, National Shrine of the Immaculate Conception

Dr. Robert B. Grogan, Organist and Carillonneur

Mrs. Virginia Brubaker, Cantor and Soloist

We gratefully acknowledge the support and contribution of:

Vietnam Veterans Assistance Fund, Incorporated

Ms. Linda Spoonster-Schwartz, President of VVAF, Inc.

6:00 P.M. Civilian Women's Service at The Wall
A Circle of Sisters-A circle of Friends

Opening and Closing prayers were offered by Reverend Beth-Marie Murphy.

7:30 P.M. Inter-Faith Service, Washington Retreat House
Women of Faith-Women of Valor

This special inter-faith service was celebrated to foster the spiritual healing of all women affected by the Vietnam War. In addition to the recognition given to the Women Veterans and Civilian Women who served in Vietnam, special recognition and attention was given to all women whose lives were touched by this war-the Wives, Mothers, Gold Star Wives, Gold Star Mothers, POW/MIA Wives, Amerasian Women and Vietnamese Women. This service was dedicated to the memory of the eight Vietnam Veteran Women and 56 Civilian Women who lost their lives in Vietnam.

Three altars were included in the service; a Christian altar, a Jewish Seder Table and a Buddhist altar. Individual portraits of the eight nurses and the Book of Honor which lists the names of the 56 Civilian Women who lost their lives in Vietnam were placed on the Christian altar. The Jewish Seder Table incorporated a special remembrance table for the POW/MIAs whose fate are still unknown.

The service was con-celebrated by the Reverend Beth-Marie Murphy of Ontario, Canada who is a Vietnam Veteran, and the Reverend Philip G. Salois, M.S.

The Call to Worship began with the playing of the song *Journeys Ended, Journeys Begun* by Weston Priory, Gregory Norbert, O.S.B.

The first reading, Judith 13:14, was proclaimed by Rita Quimby, the Mother of a Vietnam Veteran. The Responsive Reading, Judith 13:18, 19, 20, was proclaimed by Susan Schaffer, wife of NCVNVM member, Reverend Richard Schaffer.

The second reading, Esther C:12, 14-16, 23-25, was read by Geri McCabe, head Psychiatric nurse at the Boston VA Medical Center.

The Gospel, John 19:25-27, was proclaimed by Reverend Beth-Marie Murphy.

Beth-Marie delivered the homily.

A Prayer to honor the Mothers of Vietnam Veterans was read by Fr. Phil and, as he enthroned the Book of Names, the song entitled *The Wall* by Britt Small and Festival was played in their honor.

Appendix E
Origin of the Retreats
By Rev. Alan Cutter

How the Retreats Started

Our organization started as a group of spiritually wounded and frustrated Vietnam veterans seeking someone to listen; we were perhaps too mired in despair to say we hoped for some sort of healing, but I guess that's probably what we really wanted. I know I had been a church professional for several years and, while I was able to talk about many of the crises of life, no one really wanted to talk about the issue that consumed me: God and war. The first year the group, all male, gathered in Washington D.C. I am told there was a lot of just storytelling, and with the stories, often being told in a group for the first time, a lot of emotion. These men agreed that there was something good going on and that the group should continue. Somehow, bylaws and a structure appeared; I have never really asked how this happened, because I really don't care. I discovered the existence of what was called the National Conference of Viet Nam Veteran Ministers (now the International Conference of War Veteran Ministers) and decided to take a chance on it. I really needed a place to talk about God and war.

I showed up at the second Annual Conference of the group that was held in the Chicago area. A church official had forwarded to me a letter from a Catholic priest who was seeking members for this new organization of Vietnam veterans who were religious professionals. The requirements for membership were simple: ordination by some group, service in Vietnam as shown by a DD214, and fifty dollars. I got an application form, filled it out, sent copies of my certificate of ministerial standing and DD214, fifty bucks, and I was in.

I was late arriving for the conference. Introductions were going on, and I was nervous, but I'll tell you more about that later. Right now, I'm recounting how this retreat program started.

Several years after this particular meeting, the one where I first showed up, we were meeting at the Center for Christian Living in Attleboro, MA. Our group was open to hear from anyone who wanted to talk about "healing" for veterans. This particular year a group came to us from the National

Center for PTSD. The visitors, psychiatrists, psychologists, and what-have-you, shared with us information about their work and the Center. However, in the course of this conversation together something was said that caught our collective attention. It went like this: "While we have learned that combat stress can cause illness and dysfunction and while we have discovered, over the years, how to treat many of the symptoms and now have many successful treatment modalities, we have also become aware that combat, trauma, stress, PTSD is, at its very core, a wound to the human spirit, and we really don't know how to treat this. Maybe you religious folks, who deal, so you say, with the spirit, could talk about this and come up with some ways to treat wounded spirits? After all, isn't this what you do?"

Now this was quite a challenge. Actually, as religious professionals we spend the majority of our time "tending the structure" of whatever organization has commissioned us. However, it was flattering to be considered to have some expertise in tending and treating wounded souls, something we really didn't talk about that much in our daily lives and certainly something that was not highly encouraged by any of our superiors in our religious traditions. We began, as a group, to brainstorm about what we could do.

We came up with quite a list and began to divide up responsibilities to give the items a try. A few of us were intrigued by the idea of offering some sort of a healing retreat. We sat down and began to imagine a retreat weekend program, came up with a rough outline, and decided to try it. So, before we even fleshed out a real program with assignments and goals, we went to the office of the Center for Christian Living and booked a weekend for the retreat the following year. The plan called for us to begin with dinner Friday evening and conclude with Sunday lunch. In a burst of naive confidence, we decided to have a second retreat in conjunction with our next Annual Conference, which was going to be held in St. Paul, MN. Full of expectation and commitment for we had a date, those of us who were to be the leaders went home and tried to figure out exactly what we were going to do.

When the day for the retreat rolled around the following September, we had an outline of events actually printed on a piece of paper, and we had divided the labor of the weekend, each of us taking a particular segment. Since we had names for the segments and time elements it really looked as if we knew what we were doing.

We jumped in and the retreat started. After each segment, we had a coffee break; the participants would drink coffee and we leaders would caucus and critique what had just occurred and review where we were going next. To our increasing amazement the program and process we had designed seemed to be helpful, and by the end of the retreat we were stunned and relieved. It had worked.

What follows are various parts of the retreat that I have done, or helped to do, as well as brief summaries of what others did. These brief descriptions by no means take the place of an actual retreat, but perhaps they may be helpful to others on the journey.

However, first I want to share a reflection I wrote that describes my initial encounter with the members of the National Conference of War Veteran Ministers, and the story of one person who helped me on my journey.

Ambushed by Grace

In November of 1990 Father Philip Salois convened a gathering of fourteen Vietnam veterans who also happened to be religious professionals of a sort. From this gathering grew an organization known as the National Conference of Viet Nam Veteran Ministers. Phil, at that time a staff chaplain at the Boston VAMC, was a Catholic priest, a member of the Missionaries of our Lady of La Salette. But he was also a Vietnam veteran, a grunt who had been awarded a Silver Star. He had a lot to be proud of, but he was also troubled. He wanted to be able to talk about and reflect on his experience of war with his peers, but there seemed to be no one qualified to engage with him on this topic. So, Phil was given a five-minute window at a veteran gathering at "The Wall" in Washington, D.C. to promote an initial gathering of clergy who were Vietnam veterans, having either served as chaplains or having been ordained after the conflict, to explore whether or not forming a community of veterans who were clergy might be a good idea.

As the fourteen men spoke and listened to each other, they discovered that, for the first time, people who had a religious background were really listening and honoring the stories being shared. Out of that encounter grew the awareness that perhaps this group had a unique mission in helping to guide the search for meaning and spiritual healing for both the veteran community and the nation as a whole. Some of the group decided to have another meeting the next year.

That second meeting was at a Catholic retreat center in Illinois in 1991. That is when I showed up. I had read about the organization, noted a forthcoming meeting, sent in my fee, filled out the paperwork, and joined the organization.

I had recently moved to Duluth, MN, after a ten-year pastorate in West Virginia. I thought a change of scenery might alleviate the attacks of rage, flashbacks, and panic that were becoming more frequent. I convinced myself that in Duluth I would be away from the heat and humidity of the "south" and thus could avoid that "trigger" which transported me back to Vietnam. Rarely has someone so blithely stepped, as is said, "from the frying pan into the fire." Duluth had a bus system with diesel buses; the exhaust odor "triggered" memories of the large trucks in the "ammo trains." There was a factory that made wood products; their plant emitted an odor that was to me the smell of the charcoal fires of the 'villes' in Vietnam. When the first "Bush War" with Iraq broke out, I actually watched the beginning of the bombing with others during a church meeting. I was going downhill fast.

Among all the items accumulated to help acquaint me with the resources of my new community was a folder from the Duluth VET Center describing its outreach. By now I knew that much of my trouble was being caused by what had happened in Vietnam. But I was a religious professional and was the one that was supposed to give assistance, not ask for it. However, I was desperate, and in such painful turmoil that I was considering suicide. I knew I needed help. So, I began to seriously consider the VET Center.

I didn't go right away. I took some time, located it, and staked it out to see who was going in and out. Basically, old guys with beards who all looked a little bit wild. Not me. Then I looked in a mirror; son of a bitch, I had a beard! And while I didn't look wild, I knew I was always on edge, barely under control. So, one day, around Easter of 1991, a bad time for me for a variety of reasons, I went in and introduced myself. Immediately someone came to speak with me, one of the VET Center counselors, a woman. She explained that there was no free time, but she wouldn't let me leave without me making an appointment to come back soon, in a couple days. I tried to demur, but she was very nice, and quite insistent, so I made the appointment.

More than that, I even kept the appointment. This began a long series of one-on-one sessions with Cindy, who became my counselor. I hoped that I could get a Band-Aid fix and go on, another example of wishful thinking. Sometimes the appointments were incredibly painful; I had a lot of stuff I did not want to revisit. Bit by bit things began to come out. Cindy had a way of posing doorknob questions; I would have my hand literally on the doorknob ready to escape and she would ask a question and I would go to pieces emotionally. That would be where we would pick up the next time. After several months of the one-on-one sessions, Cindy suggested I join a "closed in-country group" for a twelve-week encounter. I did. I managed to maintain my usual controlled emotions until one day the leader asked a question about why I didn't go to the VA Health Clinic. Something about that triggered me and I exploded; he and the group just let me vent and work through the rage.

It was during this twelve-week period that Phil's group was meeting in Illinois. I had a commitment to the twelve-week group so I asked their permission to have a week off to go to this meeting. They granted it.

I drove over arriving a bit late; the evening session had already started. It was a round robin of sharing about who we were, when we had been in Vietnam, and where we were in life. I didn't want to say much, but I did say I had been in the Navy, in Vietnam, that I was a client of a VET Center, and I had come to learn more about what they were about. The next couple of days were incredibly hard. Everywhere I went I seemed to be ambushed by emotions or events. I had to fight to control my emotions. Thank God for bourbon. At that time, I was drinking fairly heavily and the booze helped kill the pain.

One night Phil and the others went out to visit some veterans' organizations, knowing that someone would always be willing to buy a few rounds for the "chaplains." I stayed back at the retreat center with an Episcopal priest; he had been a marine in Vietnam and lost both his legs within a few weeks of arriving there. His name was also Alan. We sat at a table and talked; he had a fifth of scotch and I had a fifth of bourbon. We had pretty well consumed our bottles when Phil and the gang rolled in. Everyone went upstairs except Phil who sat down with us to have a drink, something he needed like a hole in the head. After we had finished, we stood up as best we could. Phil suggested that before we headed upstairs, we have a prayer. So, we all sort of leaned into one another, arms around shoulders, a human tripod that was stable enough so we didn't fall. Phil offered an entirely forgettable standard prayer, but before he did, he said this, "Remember, the only thing we have to give one another is our stories." That stuck with me.

We were coming to the end of our time together, and I still hadn't said much about what was bothering me, what had happened in Vietnam. Now I am going to put together what happened from my point of view and what Phil and others have told me was happening from their side.

As I have said I asked permission to go to the meeting from the group at the Duluth VET Center, bringing to the staff the registration form, telling them about the organization, and indicating that it was fine with me if they wished to inquire to make sure everything was on the up-and-up. The VET Center Team was very open and supportive, and asked if they could share a little about the process in which I was involved. I agreed, assuming they meant to say something about the in-country group. What I did not know was that when the VET Center Team telephoned Phil, who was after all a VA chaplain and a colleague, they told him a bit about me, sharing with him a concern that I, as a religious professional, had marvelous defenses built up, and I knew too much about the methods of counseling. They inquired if he, as a colleague in faith, would try to encourage me to talk, or rather push me a little bit further "to crack me open." During the conference Phil had been trying to get me to talk more about my experience but had very little success. As time was running out, Phil decided that he would attempt a full-on assault.

That evening at supper he announced that the regular agenda would be amended; a special time of sharing would be held for he felt that not all present had taken advantage of the opportunity to share with the group. I went up to my room knowing that he was talking about me. I packed my bags and was getting ready to leave, to sneak away. Then it dawned on me that that had been my *modus operandi* for too long. I decided I would stay and tough it out.

Phil had announced that we would gather at 1930, or 7:30 pm. I went down to the meeting room at 1929. Everyone else was already there. Phil had told them to come at 1915. He had spoken to them laying just a bit of background before them, and he had primed a couple people to speak. Being a Catholic and loving all the "smells and bells" he had also set the room to create an atmosphere. The lights were dimmed, candles were lit, all were sitting in the circle; a place was reserved for me to sit on the couch between two people. He had even chosen music for the evening. After an opening explanation that this was an evening of open sharing and that the one speaking would speak until he was finished, a repeat of the first evening's instructions, he played one of the pieces he had selected.

One of the group shared something, and then another. There was an interlude in which Phil played another of his chosen selections; this time I recall it was the prayer from **Les Mis** that includes the sentiments "bring him home" and "let him live." I was writhing on the couch in spiritual agony while this was going on. Then a fellow that Phil had asked to speak did his bit to increase my discomfort; he shared his own story of fleeing from the horrors. More music from *Les Mis*: "empty chairs at empty tables . . . my friends, forgive me that I live and you are gone." That really touched every tender spot I had been keeping hidden. The music ended; the room was silent; Phil, from his seat directly across the room, looked intently at me and raised his eyebrows.

I said to myself, "Oh fuck it!" I threw my glasses down on the table in front of me, leaned forward, and said something to the effect of "Let me tell you what happened to the people I was closest to in Vietnam." My own memory was that I was concise and spoke for about five minutes. The rest of the group assures me that I talked for almost an hour. Without going into the details, suffice it to say that I spoke of loneliness and loss, abandonment and betrayal, and death, the latter caused by my hand.

When I finished, I was exhausted and I sat back and closed my eyes. My story put me so far outside the realm of acceptable behavior that I was sure that I was a dead man, that this righteous group would kill me now for I knew I deserved it. So, I waited for death. It didn't happen.

Instead, I opened my eyes and, on the table, appeared bread and wine. Together we celebrated the Lord's Supper. I was confused but was aware of a great sense of personal relief. It would take a long time for me to sort it all out; I am still working at it.

The next morning when I came down to breakfast the men in the group were looking at me with interest. I didn't think much of it at the time. Phil told me later that they were fascinated by the change in my face, from twisted to relaxed, from a portrait of agony to a face with hope. A few years later, at a conference when we were discussing moments when lives had changed, one of the members who had been in Des Plaines turned and said to me, "You scared the shit out of me when you spoke!" He went on to say that, after I had shared my story, some of them had gathered wondering how they could help me. Phil had told them that they had done what they could, that it was up to me, and they would know that something good had happened if I showed up at the next conference. I did and have not missed one in over twenty years.

The conferences have been my reunion, my checkpoint, every year. Some people count years by birthdays, or holidays; I mark the year by conference dates. And here let me pat myself on the back. Once I started down the pathway of healing, I decided I would always keep going and never be satisfied with where I was. It was tempting to stop for the fear was there that, if I kept going, I might lose the sense of healing I had achieved; there could by a mighty, dark, deep pit ahead. But I have kept going; I have hit bumps along the way, but there has always been enough light to let me go forward.

Appendix F
Flier Soliciting Chaplains in the Armed Forces to Join The National Conference of Vietnam Veteran Ministers

Chaplain in the Armed Forces?
Ordained after your service?

Come join us!

We are a
welcoming community
of wounded healers sharing
our experiences
of war
and
its aftermath.

The Beginning

In November of 1990 Father Philip Salois convened a gathering of four-teen Vietnam veterans who also happened to be religious profession-als of a sort. From this gathering grew an organization known as the National Conference of Viet Nam Veteran Ministers. Phil, a priest of the Missionaries of our Lady of La Salette, was at that time a staff chaplain at the Boston Veterans Administration Medical Center. But he was also a Vietnam veteran, an infantry "grunt" who had been awarded a Silver Star. He had a lot to be proud of, but he was also troubled. He wanted to be able to talk about and reflect on his experience of war with his peers, but there seemed to be no one qualified to engage with him on this topic. So, Phil was given a five-minute window at a veterans' gathering at "The Wall" in Washington, D.C. to promote an initial gathering of clergy who were Vietnam veterans, having either served as chaplains or having been ordained after the conflict, to explore whether or not forming a community of veterans who were clergy might be a good idea.

As the fourteen men spoke and listened to each other, they discovered that, for the first time, people who had a religious background were really listening and honoring the stories being shared.

Out of that encounter grew an awareness that perhaps this group might have a unique mission in helping guide the search for meaning and spiritual healing for both the veteran community and the nation as a whole. Some of the group decided to have another meeting the next year.

One Story

Our organization started as a group of spiritually wounded and frustrated Vietnam veterans seeking someone to listen; we were perhaps too mired in despair to say we hoped for some sort of healing, but I guess that's probably what we really wanted. I know I had been a church professional for a number of years and, while I was able to talk about many of the crises of life, no one really wanted to talk about the issue that consumed me: God and war.

The first year the group, all male, gathered in Washington D.C. I am told there was a lot of just story-telling, and with the stories, often being told in a group for the first time, a lot of emotion. These men agreed that there was something good going on and that the group should continue. Somehow, bylaws and a structure appeared; I have never really asked how this happened, because I really don't care. I discovered the existence of what was called the National Conference of Viet Nam Veteran Ministers (now the International Conference of War Veteran Ministers) and decided to take a chance on it. I really needed a place to talk about God and war.

I showed up at the second Annual Conference of the group that was held in the Chicago area at a Catholic Retreat Center. A church official had forwarded to me a letter from a Catholic priest who was seeking members for this new organization of Vietnam veterans who were now religious professionals.

The requirements for membership were simple: ordination by some group, service in Vietnam as shown by a DD214 (certificate of Discharge from Active-Duty listing assignments, training, and awards as well as other information), and fifty dollars. I got an application form, filled it out, sent copies of my certificate of ministerial standing and DD214, fifty bucks, and I was in.

Membership

Back in the olden days, when this organization began, we were all Vietnam veterans who were male, ordained clergy. Some of the group had been chaplains; others served in various capacities in Vietnam and were later ordained to ministry. Our common bond was that somehow our experience in Vietnam had changed us, leaving us with a wound in our spirits, and we needed to reflect upon that change with people willing to simply listen. Within our various denominational entities, we found no one willing to do so.

Over the years our membership has evolved in wonderful ways. Realizing that we had not only brothers in Vietnam and in ministry but also sisters who had served and were now in ministry, we welcomed these veterans into our group. Then we realized that the United States had allies in Vietnam and so we began to welcome veterans who were now religious professionals in Canada, Australia, and New Zealand. To our dismay war became almost a constant in our lives and world, so we opened our membership to veterans working in ministry who had served and were serving in other conflicts. And we extended our outreach to various veterans' organizations around the world. Our group was enriched by members from Great Britain and Ireland.

Our membership is still evolving! An experience of war or an interest in working with war trauma and $50 (that hasn't changed!) will get you a year's membership in the ICWVM.

The Annual Conference:
Building Community

One of the objectives of the International Conference of War Veteran Ministers has beenbuilding a community where the members and others can come together and, putting aside denomination difference and disagreements, focus on listening to one another, accepting the gifts of each other's stories, and celebrating the deep affection that binds us together.

Admittedly the core background of the membership has been the Judeo-Christian tradition, but being in this tradition is by no means a barrier to others coming to be with us. We have found that there is much in all faith traditions to enjoythat is in common; one of the common traits is the emphasis of being together in **community**.

The yearly Annual Conference is our basic building block for establishing our community. We purposely try to gather in different parts of the country so that members who may not wish to travel from coast to coast have an opportunity to attend. Many years we have met at Catholic Retreat houses, but we have enjoyed hospitality at a number of different venues as well. OurConference allows time for sharing stories, learning something new, and playing together, often featuring a field trip and always an evening meal at a fine dining establishment. And we do not neglect our need for feeding our spirits as wehave enjoyed a variety of devotional experiences led by our members.

Meet just a few of our members:
Father Philip Salois, a priest of the Missionaries of Our Lady of La Salette, who has recently retired as Chief of Chaplain Service for the VA Boston Healthcare System. Phil is the founder of the National Conference of Viet Nam Veteran Ministers (now the International Conference of War Veteran Ministers. He had been an Army soldier (199th Light Infantry Brigade) in Vietnam serving in the "boonies" in III Corps.

Rev. Dr. Jackson Day isapastor of the United Methodist Church, a consultant for Health Care Advocacy with the United Methodist General Board of Church and Society, in his "retirement" an active pastor at Providence United Methodist Church (Towson, MD), and Executive Director of the International Conference of War Veteran Ministers. Jack had been an Army chaplain with the First Brigade, 4th Infantry Division, in the Central Highlands, II Corps.

Sister Linda McClenahan isa member of the Racine (WI) Dominican Sisters, a licensed counselor working with people suffering from post-traumatic stress, and first vice-president of the International Conference of War Veteran Ministers. Sister Linda was a staff sergeant assigned to the 1st Signal Brigade in Long Binh.

Rev. Dr. Alan Cutter is a pastor of the Presbyterian Church (USA), now happily retired. Currently he is the President of the International Conference of War Veteran Ministers. Alan spent five years on active duty in the Navy. As an enlisted man he was in the Naval Security Group where he learned North Vietnamese. As a newly commissioned Ensign in 1972, he was sent to Vietnam to operate around Danang and points North "accordingto the needs of the service."

Mission/Projects

Over the years The ICWVM has had several majorprojects in order to fulfill our mission of being a resource for the veteran community. One of our ongoing projects is our Annual Conference, but we have also had a few other special projects. Read about them here!

Our members and friends have also had projects they have undertaken. Some of them have published books. So, we have here a booklist as well.

VVA Book of Prayers and Services

At the request of Vietnam Veterans of America National Chaplain Philip Salois and in fulfillment of our organization's mission to help guide the search for meaning for both the veteran community and the nation at large, we created a **Book of Prayers and Services** for VVA Chapters and Chaplains. It contained suggested services for Memorial Day and Veterans Day as well as services of remembrance for those missing in action or recently deceased. Rituals for installation of officers as well as disposing of colors were included. In addition to other materials, three specific sections of prayers were included which we felt addressed the particular concerns of Vietnam veterans, and which also address common concerns of all other war veterans; these prayers address the reality of suffering, the hope for true friendship, and the quest for peace. The editor for this project was Alan Cutter.

Risking Connection in Faith Communities

This curriculum was originally created for working with survivors of child abuse, was funded by the State of Maine, and developed by the Sidran Institute in collaboration with Trauma Research, Education, and Training Institute of South Windsor, CT. The National Conference of Viet Nam Veteran Ministers (now the ICWVM) grasped the importance of making the insights of the original curriculum available to clergy in addressing not only war trauma but all trauma experiences; and, in partnership with Sidran, obtained grants for planning and implementation from the E. Rhodes and Leona B. Carpenter Foundation to fund this adaptation of the material to extend its scope to all experiences of trauma. Because it is intended for leaders of faith communities, this curriculum makes one significant departure from the original: it assumes the reality of God in the lives of its readers and treats connection with God as a significant aspect of healing from trauma. Intended to be useful to clergy of the major religions and denominations, all characterizations of God from any faith perspective were used only illustratively to sidebar examples and scenarios. The NCVNVM (now ICWVM) representative on this project was Jackson Day.

The Spiritual Retreats

At one of our Annual Conferences, we hosted representatives from the National Center for PTSD shared with us information about their work and discoveries. They shared something with us that caught our collective attention. It went something like this: "While we have learned that combat stress can cause illness and dysfunction and while we have discovered, over the years, how to treat many of the symptoms and now have many successful treatment modalities, we have also become aware that combat, trauma, stress, PTSD is, at its very core, a wound to the human spirit, and we really don't know how to treat this. Maybe you religious folks, who deal, so you say, with the spirit, could talk about this and come up with some ways to treat wounded spirits? After all, isn't this what you do?" Now this was quite a challenge. Actually, as religious professionals we spend the majority of our time "tending the structure" of whatever organization has commissioned us. However, it was flattering to be considered to have some expertise in tending and treating wounded souls, something we really didn't talk about that much in our daily lives and certainly something that was not highly encouraged by any of our superiors in our religious traditions. But then some of our organization decided to take up the challenge and create a healing retreat program.

The first retreat was an adventure. The leadership team included Phil Salois, Jack Day, and Alan Cutter. We were joined by Vietnam author and spouse Patience Mason. We had an agenda,a few ideas, and our own experiences. Without going into a lot of detail, we discovered that our retreat format worked, and we began to treat in our gathering what we came to call Post Traumatic **Spiritual** Disorder. Over the yearswe have developed several patterns and much materialthat we are willing to share and have shared with the Veterans Administration, at conferences of the International Society of Traumatic StressStudies, and at other places where we have been invited to speak. We are still willing to do so.

You will note that there are no pictures in this section. Part of the retreat process was creating a space of complete safety so we will take no chance that, even by a picture, we might reveal some of the participants. Building trust was an important part of the process, and we will not endanger that trust that we share with other veterans.

ICWVM Booklist

Over the years a number of our presenters, friends, and members have written about their experiences. We share here some of the books that have been written by this group. The books may be found by using search engines, or by going to Amazon.

Books Sponsored by ICWVM:

Risking Connection in Faith Communities – Sidran Institute, Jack Day and others

VVA Ritual Book – Alan Cutter, editor

Books by Members, Presenters, and Friends

Ron Camarda – *Tear in the Desert*

Allen Clark – *Wounded Soldier, Healing Warrior*
   Valor in Vietnam 1963-1977:
   Chronicles of Honor, Courage and Sacrifice

Alan Cutter – *Hope and Healing for Veterans*

   The Alphabet of God, War, and Hope
   God's Story, My Story
   At the Altar of War

Walter Davis – *Shattered Dream*

Chuck Dean – *Nam Vet: Making Peace with Your Past*
   Walking Point: A Spiritual Journey for Warriors
   and others

Robert Gran – *The Way of the Wound*

David Grossman – *On Killing*

Kermit Johnson – *Ethics and Counterrevolution*

Alistair Little – *Give A Boy a Gun*

Bill Mahedy – *Out of the Night*

Patience Mason – *Recovering From the War*

Robert Mason – *Chickenhawk*
   Chickenhawk: Back in the World

Aphrodite Matsakis – *Vietnam Wives*

Michael Muller, aka Michael FitzGordon – *A Dream of Heaven*

Nigel Mumford – *Hand to Hand: From Combat to Healing*
    The Forgotten Touch
    After the Trauma the Battle Begins

Uwe Simeon-Netto – *The Acquittal of God*

Barry and Sandra Pearce – *Geelong to Nui Dat and Back*

Robert Reilly – *Return of the Warriors: Vietnam War Veterans Face the Ghosts of Their Past on Their Personal Battlegrounds.*

Jonathan Shay – *Achilles in Vietnam*
    Odysseus in America

Carey Spearman – *Vietnam Veterans Homecoming:*
    Crossing the Line

Claude Thomas – *At Hell's Gate*

Edward Tick – *War and the Soul*

Lynda VanDeVanter, Joan Furey – *Visions of War, Dreams of Peace*

Martin Webster – *Soldier of Consequence*
    Diary of a Disgraced Soldier (video)

Appendix G
Full Text of Fr. Phil's Speech in Tbilisi

Journey From Darkness to Light
Spirituality as a Vehicle for Healing

I have discovered in the last twenty years how powerful and important our personal stories are to restore us to wholeness and bring us to a greater sense of inner peace. Once we have mustered up the courage to take a long, hard look at ourselves in the mirror without disgust – without shame – without turning away – then we begin to experience the journey from darkness into light. We would have fought in wars – experienced death and destruction on the battlefield – engaged in killing and maiming – lost buddies close to us – lost legs and arms or other body parts – been separated from our loved ones because of war – these are not only examples of physical and emotional pain, but equally as important – spiritual injury – devastation of our soul.

For thirteen years I carried the spiritual and emotional wounds of war from my year in Vietnam. I buried those feelings for all those years. In America, we were not given permission to talk or think about the war. It was shunned by society and a scourge on the minds of the American people. We won every battle but lost the war. Our older veterans of World War II kept reminding us that we lost the war and were not welcome in their veteran organizations. We were ridiculed by the way we looked – the way we dressed – the way we behaved. We were not received back into our country with cheers but with jeers. We were called names like, "murderer" "baby-killer" "cry-babies" and the list goes on ad infinitum. We could not find work if we mentioned that we fought in Vietnam. Our old friends from school who went to college and university instead of joining the Armed Forces did not want to associate with us anymore. Although we were only gone one year to Vietnam, things were so different when we returned that it could not have been more different than had we landed on the planet Mars. Who had changed? The folks at home or the soldiers coming back from war? We thought the folks at home had changed – they had changed but not nearly as much as we did upon returning home. Many family members and friends told us they no longer knew who we were.

I have discovered my true self through my story. It took a long time to embrace that story because it was not neat and pretty but one that carried with it a lot of pain and emotional scars. I did not discover my story alone because it was so painful. I needed to enter into a therapeutic relationship with a professional counselor who was also a Vietnam combat veteran. I needed to establish a trusting relationship with that man before I could begin to open my heart and soul to him.

The one major incident that occurred in Vietnam has become the catharses for my healing and has become the focal point for my Sacred Story – my *Journey from Darkness to Light*. I use the word sacred because it is my story – it is unique – it belongs to no one else – it is a gift. God made me unique – a miraculous combination of genes and there is no one else on Earth with the same blueprint. That is why I am sacred, and the sacredness of my story is a gift from God. It is He who blesses me and makes me worthy and holy.

The turning point in my story begins on March 1, 1970, in the triple – We were company size on a search and destroy mission looking for a battalion size North Vietnamese Army bunker complex. We found them late in the afternoon on February 28, 1970. It was too late in the day to engage the enemy. Darkness falls early in triple canopy jungle. The order came down from the Command Center that we would set off in the opposite direction for 2,000 meters and set up a defensive perimeter for the night. Canopy jungle of War Zone D in the Republic of South Vietnam. I was a Private in an infantry unit – 199 Light Infantry Brigade – A Company – 3rd Battalion – 7th Infantry. I was in the Second Platoon. The plan was we would break up camp early the next morning and the Second Platoon – my platoon would lead the company out to pursue the enemy and destroy them. Early the next morning of 1 March 1970, we proceeded as planned. We broke up camp early and Second Platoon led out the company. The Company Commander made the ultimate error in his haste to get in and get the job done. He ordered us down the same trail we had marched up on the evening before when we had found the NVA bunker complex. The enemy knew our position and were waiting for us as we approached. We walked right into a U-shaped ambush – surrounded on three sides by the enemy. We were receiving fire from three sides, and we immediately set up a defensive front to return the fire. Chaos broke out until we could get our bearings on where the fire was coming from. In the melee, we noticed that the forward element of our platoon was separated from us by a twenty-yard clearing. There were six men in that forward element: the Point man; Compass man; Pace man;

the Platoon leader (1ˢᵗ Lieutenant Terrence Bowell) and his RTO (the Radio Operator) and one other soldier.

Time seemed to stand still while we were in the middle of the firefight. I cannot recall how much time elapsed except that for me it seemed as if much time had elapsed when I noticed that no real efforts were being made to rescue the separated forward element. This made me very angry and so in the midst of this firefight I said a very brief prayer to God that went something like this:

"God, I am going out there to rescue these guys. If you bring me back safe and sound without a scratch, I will do anything you want."

I never remembered that promise after I muttered it. Nor did I promise that I would become a priest.

I then went to the berm where we had set up our defensive line and told my buddies there that I was going to make a run out there to rescue our men. It was a crazy and foolhardy idea. Everyone thought so. They tried to dissuade me. Nothing doing. I was not going to be dissuaded. I was not interested in playing the hero – it was not my style – it was sheer rage from knowing our men were out there and no one was making any moves to rescue them. I remember saying to myself that if I was out there, I would have wanted someone to come to help me. We had lost radio contact with the Radio Man in the front. That meant the radio had been shot up or that the Radio Man was dead. Another buddy by the name Herbert Klug came up to me and said that if I was going to do this crazy thing, that he would come with me. He devised the plan, and the plan was this: about halfway out in the clearing there was a huge boulder large enough to provide cover for the two of us. We would make a move out to that boulder and spray the entire right flank with firepower to divert the enemy's attention from the men of the separated element. This would enable the members of the separated element to make a run back to the line of defense. The plan was a go. A third man, Edmund "Killer" Killingbeck, decided to jump on board our little rescue operation. Killingbeck received a shoulder wound and had to retreat immediately to the rear. Klug and I made a dash out to the boulder and completed the mission as planned. One by one, we saw four of the soldiers make a run for safety behind the defensive line. When we saw there was no more activity, Herb decided it was time for us to make a run back to the line. We both low-crawled back shoulder-to-shoulder – eyes focused straight ahead to the line of safety. I made it back safely and when I turned around to look for Klug he was nowhere to be found.

I asked the guys where he was, they told me he did not come back with me. I said, "What do you mean, he didn't come back? He was right next to me." I was so focused on crawling back to safety I had not noticed that he was no longer at my side. When I looked over the berm, I saw Klug sprawled out on his stomach about halfway out. Without thinking and still under fire, I ran back out to Klug to bring him in. I could not even budge him an inch – he was so heavy. I couldn't understand why he was so heavy. When some of the others saw me struggling with bringing Klug back, two soldiers came out and helped me drag him in. After we brought Klug back behind the line, we turned him over and found that he had received a clean rifle wound in the chin that went through the top of his head. He was killed immediately. He never knew what hit him.

No time to grieve for my buddy, there were still two men who had not returned from the front. The guys asked me if I would go out a third time to help them locate the exact positions of the two soldiers. I brought a small squad with me, and we located the two soldiers. One was the Radio Man who was so wounded, he could not move. They brought him back on a litter. The other man was our Platoon Leader, 1st Lieutenant Terrance Bowell who was also killed.

By the end of the day, we had two killed in action and eighteen wounded and were flown out by Medevac helicopters. There were only seven of us left in the platoon who were not hit and I was one of them. We were not able to go too far to set up our nighttime perimeter because we were engaged in battle for the better part of March 1st. That night when darkness fell, I was terror-filled. I was convinced in my mind that the enemy would come back in the middle of the night and finish us off. The events of the day never ceased to repeat themselves in my mind. Every detail had been burned into my memory.

The Vietnam Closed
When I came home after one year and twelve days, it was like entering a new planet. Within 48 hours I was whisked out of Vietnam and brought to the Oakland Army Base to process out and jumped on a plane to Los Angeles to come home to my parents. I went back to work and quickly forgot about Vietnam at least on the surface. I soon found out the hard way that nobody or very few wanted to know about my experiences in Vietnam. They were happy that I had returned but did not want to hear my accounts of the war. It got stuffed deep down inside for some 13 years.

In May 1972 I felt a call to the Priesthood. I entered the Seminary in the Fall semester and began my course of studies and discernment. In October 1974, on a sunny autumn afternoon about 5:00 P.M. I had been studying for the Priesthood and living the Seminary life and very content with my life-choice. I remember at the time thanking God for calling me to the Priesthood while praying my Rosary. Then I heard that inner voice, which I firmly believe was the voice of God say to me, *"Do you remember the promise you made to me, four years ago on March 1ˢᵗ, 1970 in Vietnam that if I got you out of this mess safe and sound without a scratch, you would do anything I wanted? Well, this is what I want for you."* It was a most powerful experience for me because that was the **FIRST TIME** I had remembered that battlefield promise since I had uttered it in a desperate time in my life in the jungles of Vietnam. It gave me the assurance that I needed to continue on this long journey to the Priesthood. I have never regretted that decision although it has not been easy all these years. The remarkable thing for me was to know that I did not enter the Seminary in 1972 to pay off a debt from a promise I had made to God in Vietnam since I had no recollection of that promise after that tragic event. God waited until I was settled and at peace before reminding me of that promise. He obviously had a plan for me that has only been revealed to me years later – that Vietnam would become a life-giving experience that would enrich my Priesthood and be of service to other victims of war.

But the silence of Vietnam remained only in my mind and in my soul unknown to others.

"THE WALL – The Vietnam Veterans Memorial"

In 1977, I entered a religious congregation, the Congregation of the Missionaries of Our Lady of La Salette in Massachusetts. I wanted to live in a religious community. The selection of this community I believe was also providential. Our Lady of La Salette had appeared to two small uneducated children in the French Alps on September 19, 1846, as the *"Virgin of Tears"* or the *"Weeping Mother."* She presented a model theme for ministry for the Religious Congregations – the Charism of Reconciliation. This has become the primary focus of our community and essentially my ministry. As people who have suffered in whatever manner, we reach out to people who have suffered in whatever shape or form that suffering comes. For me, it has been in the area of war veterans and their families that the direction my priestly ministry has taken.

In 1983, I had finished my formal studies for the Priesthood and was an ordained Deacon in the Roman Catholic Church. I was serving in a La Salette parish in New Hampshire when I received a brochure in the mail. It was entitled, *"Ministering to the Vietnam Veteran – A Workshop for Ministers.* "It was sponsored by the local Vietnam Veteran Center. The purpose of this workshop was to teach non-veteran clergy the unique and specific spiritual needs of the Vietnam Veteran. I attended this Minister's workshop. There were about twenty area ministers in attendance. There was a panel of seven Vietnam Combat Veterans who one by one began to tell their personal stories of Vietnam and the turn their lives took after the war. I went there really believing I was going to be the teacher/minister ready to heal their hurts. What really happened was the opposite. As I listened intently to each of their painful, tragic war stories I was sent right back into Vietnam in the middle of the jungles. I lost all sense of being in that room – I was reliving all the painful and frightful event of my tour in Vietnam. I was on the verge of tears for much of the day. I felt sick in my stomach. I felt like running out of the room and never coming back – but part of me did not want to create a scene so I toughed it out and stayed. By the end of the day, I was a mess. It must have been very obvious that I was not faring well when one of the Vietnam Veteran panelists came up to me and asked, *"Are you all right?"* I replied, *"I don't think so. I don't know what it is, but I am feeling pretty awful."* He then asked if I would like to come in and see him to talk about it. I said that I would, and I went home. That night was a sleepless one for me. I kept thinking about Vietnam and everything that had transpired that day. So I called John Brock the very next day to set up an appointment and he told me to come in right away. I did not expect to see him so soon. But it was just what the doctor ordered as I committed to enter into a therapeutic relationship with John for the next six months. He happened to be an ordained minister of God. I felt comfortable with John and began to trust him with my darkest secrets and my feelings which were pretty raw at the time. It was a long and painful retelling of my Vietnam story. Many parts I could not remember but the more time passed the more it began to come back little by little. After all it was thirteen years after I had left Vietnam that I entered into PTSD counseling.

At the end of the six months, John told me I would have to go the Vietnam Veteran Memorial in Washington, DC otherwise known as **The Wall**. I was ordained a Priest on June 4, 1984, and on July 4th I went to The Wall for the first time to look up the name of my buddy, Herbert Wheeler Klug (Panel 13-West; Line 71) I said a prayer and passed my hand over the indentation of his name on that cold, shiny, black granite wall. It was a significant benchmark in my healing story.

1990 – The Landmark Year of Healing

There were two significant events that occurred in 1990 that virtually have changed my life and have given me new life.

In the previous year, 1989, I was given a book to read, entitled *Out of the Night: A Spirituality for Vietnam Veterans* by William P. Mahedy who was a Catholic Chaplain in Vietnam. It was the first book ever written on the subject of the Vietnam War with a focus on spiritual healing. I could not put the book down and I realized that I would have to invite Vietnam into my spirituality and religious life and turn that curse into a blessing. One night after having finished the book, I felt a strong urge to find Reverend Mahedy and call him. I got to thinking that I must not be the only priest in the United States that served in the war as a soldier carrying a weapon and trained to kill the enemy. I felt that I had no community that I could turn to with my issues of war and reconciling what I did then to my Priesthood now. My fellow Vietnam Veterans came to me for counseling and advice so I could not very well burden them with my thoughts and feelings when they were coming to me for help. My religious community – fellow priests and brothers – could not understand why Vietnam was still such a problem for me. They empathized to a certain degree but could not understand. They kept telling me, *"Phil, the war was twenty years ago – haven't you gotten over it yet? Get on with your life! The past is past! Don't dwell on the past!"* These are idioms that I used to hear over and over again. So, I swallowed everything and did not talk about Vietnam to anyone who could not understand. Unless you have been in a war, you can never understand. That is why it was so important for me to find other priests and ministers like myself, to help me heal and to share my struggles living in a religious life.

I did call Reverend Mahedy the next day and told him about my idea to find other clergy who served in the Vietnam War as soldiers, sailors, or airmen. My plan was to locate enough of them and invite them to come to a conference/retreat in Washington, DC. I was hoping that Reverend Mahedy would take the idea and with it do the work for me. He replied what an excellent idea it was and that I should spearhead the project. Well, that idea backfired right back into my lap. I did not know where to begin and yet I believed I needed such a group to relate with and to heal from the trauma of war.

I decided to write a letter to Jan Scruggs, a Vietnam Combat Veteran who had served in the same military brigade I did, although I never knew him in Vietnam. Jan Scruggs was the man who dreamed a dream that the dead soldiers of the Vietnam War needed to be remembered. He was the prime-mover behind the building of The Wall, in Washington, DC. And so, I wrote to him about my idea to establish a National Conference of Vietnam Veteran Ministers and to see if he had any ideas how I could go about this. Never expecting to hear from him he called me at work one day to tell me he really liked the idea of what I was trying to do and that if I went down to Washington, DC for Veterans Day (November 11) in 1989, he would give me five minutes to speak to the 3,000-person gathering. He assured me that many people would come up to me after the ceremony to give me names and addresses of clergy who either served in Vietnam as Chaplains or as enlisted men. Sure enough, I did that and it happened just as he said. I collected many leads into clergy who were Vietnam veterans. I announced my plans and told the people gathered that this time next year – 1990, I would hold my first Annual conference of the National Conference of Viet Nam Veteran Ministers in Washington, DC.

When I returned to Boston after that Veterans Day, I began to work hard at writing to those leads asking for other leads. I sent hundreds of letters to religious authorities of all denominations requesting they forward my letter to any potential clergy member who was a Vietnam veteran that might have interest in NCVNVM.

After a lot of hard work and planning, I had accumulated quite a list of clergy who were Vietnam veterans. It took a long time of coaxing to persuade many of them to take the risk of coming to such a conference not knowing what they would expect. Our first meeting was in Washington, DC and we had twenty-two Vietnam veteran clergy present in November 1990 around Veterans Day – November 11th. Our main agenda for the first annual meeting was storytelling. We took three full days to go around to each clergy to tell their Vietnam story through the eyes of religious faith. It was such as powerful, tearful and bonding moment among all those present. We began the long process of healing ourselves – healing the healers – through the powerful presence of the Holy Spirit of God. There was no mistaking that God was in the center of each and every one of those stories. We have met every year since 1990 in a different locality in the United States and always in a religious retreat house. We have lost some members who felt they got what they needed from the conference, and we have gained many new members as well throughout the years.

The other benchmark experience of 1990 for me was the **FULL-CIRCLE PROJECT**. Ever since the war, I had always carried a deep mistrust and profound dislike for Vietnamese people that really translated to all oriental peoples. As a priest, it was such a contradiction for me to harbor such deep resentments and hatred. When the opportunity arose from the University of Massachusetts through the William Joiner Center for the Study of War and Its Social Consequences conjointly with the National Center for PTSD at the Boston Veterans Affairs Medical Center to take part in the **FULL-CIRCLE PROJECT**, I really felt that I needed to do this in order to further my journey to healing and peace of mind. The Full-Circle Project was a psychological research project designed to send a group of Vietnam veterans back to Vietnam to revisit their battlefields and to study the results of whether it was therapeutic to bring veterans back to their areas of operations. I decided to volunteer for this program. I was selected to be one of twelve Vietnam veterans of which one was a woman veteran – a nurse who served in an evacuation hospital. It was a frightening thing for all of us – I was certainly no exception. The trip was for three weeks in June 1990 beginning in the north at Hanoi and ending up in Ho Chi Minh City daily. We visited not only our own areas of operations but also sites of famous battles and sites that hold a lot of pain and shame like My Lai. One of the major factors that hit me on this return trip to Vietnam was the awful heat and humidity; the stench of the land I remembered from twenty years prior; the armed military with the AK47 rifles and pith helmets in Hanoi. I just could not look at the men – I always looked at them as the enemy or someone I may have fought against in the war. The breakthrough was the little children. Everywhere we went the children came running around us – touching us – talking and laughing at us. It was the thought that these children had never known what war was, that got me to loosen up a bit and enjoy their sheer innocence and playfulness. It was through the children that I began to look at the men with new eyes and, as I loosened up, was eventually able to let go of the hatred, resentment and mistrust of the Vietnamese.

My battle area was at the end of the trip in the southern portion of Vietnam in Xuan Loc. I wanted to bury the bracelet bearing Herbert Klug's name on it as a way of honoring his memory and the sacrifice he paid with his life to save others. There was such a torrential monsoon that day that I could not get near the place where we served. The next day we were in Ho Chi Minh City, and we were only going to be in Vietnam for three more days before returning home. I felt that my personal plan for healing was foiled because of the weather. I was very frustrated. In Saigon, I went to visit the Roman Catholic Cathedral of Notre-Dame and met the Rector of the Cathedral and asked him if I could concelebrate a Mass with him. He invited me to return the next day to concelebrate with him. I was so thrilled. I found out that I was only the second American priest to celebrate Mass in that Cathedral and the first Priest who was a soldier in the war. He asked me to share some thoughts with the people. I spoke French to the people and the Rector simultaneously translated in Vietnamese. There were about 200-300 worshippers and yet it was only a daily Mass. I told them who I was and how I participated in the war twenty years prior as a soldier killing and my men getting killed and wounded. I needed to ask their forgiveness for my participation in the war and for the pain it caused them. Likewise, I needed to forgive them for the pain it inflicted on America, its people, and its soldiers. After Holy Communion, I sat down and reflected on the magnificence of this Cathedral Church, and I began to think, *"Who would have thought that twenty years ago I was in the jungles only 65 miles away from here shooting at these people, that twenty years later almost to the day that I would be sitting in this Church concelebrating a Mass of Thanksgiving and Reconciliation for these same people."* That revelation was the cathartic healing moment on that pilgrimage. God chose not to heal me in Xuan Loc the day before but brought me farther – transcending the Xuan Loc experience into His house to bestow His special healing blessing on me. It was a real epiphany moment for me.

Another amazing thing that happened as a result of my participation in the Mass was a visit to my hotel that evening from a Vietnamese man and his daughter. He only spoke French and Vietnamese and I only spoke English and French so French became our communication vehicle. He and his family were at the Mass I had concelebrated and listened to what I said. He came looking for a special favor. He told me that he had been a professor of French in the school system but after the war the communist government stripped him of his teaching faculties – his sole way of supporting his family. He was reduced to being a street vendor scraping a meager wage for his family. He had adopted two throwaway children – Amerasian children – a boy and a girl – children of a Vietnamese mother and American GI father. For ten long years, he had attempted to reestablish his family to the United States under the Orderly Departure Program in Bangkok. Somehow his paperwork had been lost or buried under a pile of other petitioners on someone's desk in Bangkok. He asked me if I could help him by writing to the ODP program in Bangkok upon my return to the States and help them come to the US. I did write a letter and behold, their paperwork was found and the process of granting them refugee status began. They were sent to the Philippines for six months of orientation and learning basic skills in the English language. They needed sponsors and so I adopted this family of six – a mother, a father, and four adult children, three daughters and a son. They arrived in the US in September of 1992 and today in 1999 they have all become US citizens except for the mother, speak English and are all gainfully employed. They have a beautiful home with a large van to transport themselves. It was healing for them and for me. I was able to bring part of my Vietnam experience home to America. They are my adopted family and they still to this day call me "Papa."

1991—The Missing Link

The establishment of the National Conference of Vietnam Veteran Ministers and the return Pilgrimage to Vietnam were benchmarks of healing moments for me, but there was still an important link that was missing in that chain of events I call my *Pilgrimage of Healing.* There was a man in Texas by the name of B.G. Burkett, nicknamed "Jug." He served in Vietnam in the same Brigade as me—199th Light Infantry Brigade, although at a different time and place. I had not and still have not ever seen him face-to-face. He was on a crusade to expose *"wannabe"* veterans. (*"Wannabe"* veterans are those who claim to be veterans and fabricate elaborate stories to be in the spotlight or to make themselves important and needed. They are impostors.) He had read my story in a national publication and in that story related the account of the March 1st rescue mission and my being awarded the third highest medal for valor—the Silver Star. He found my phone number one day to let me know that he had read my story and wanted to verify that I was telling the truth and whether I had indeed earned the Silver Star. I was taken aback by his intrusiveness and belligerence, so I offered to send him a copy of my Silver Star citation if it was any of his business. He said not to bother, since through the Freedom of Information Act, he had sent away for my Military records through the Department of the Army. I was shocked at this behavior and he reminded me that he was acting within the law and had the right to do so. Knowing that I was upset, he asked me if I had ever been in touch with Herb Klug's family. I told him no, that I did not know how to get a hold of them. I only knew that Herb was from Dayton, Ohio, but I never made an effort to find them. He told me that I should, that it would be important to do so. I politely said yes, maybe one day I will do that. Then we said good-bye thinking that that would be the last I heard from 'Jug." A couple of weeks went by when I received a letter from Texas, only to find out that it was from "Jug." I opened it only to discover a short note from him thanking me for talking to him over the phone and a phone number. The note read: "Here is the telephone number for Herb's parents in case you want to call them." I was angry at him because now I had a phone number, no address that would have provided greater safety in writing than telephoning. What would I say to these people after twenty-one years that I never once tried to reach out to them to comfort them or tell them I served proudly with their son. I sat on that phone number for two whole weeks. It was burning a hole in my soul. I thought about that phone number day and night. It gave me no rest, no peace of mind. Finally, one morning I mustered enough courage to call these perfect strangers. I had one hand placed on the hook switch intending to hang up if anyone answered the phone. I punched the numbers on the phone. It rang several times and then I heard a man's voice answer the phone and I could not hang up on the man. I proceeded to ask him a series of questions: *"Is this Mr. Klug I am speaking to? It is. Did you have a son named Herb? I did. Was he killed in Vietnam? He was."* Then I said to him, *"I do not want you to think that this is a crank call or some terrible practical joke. I just wanted to tell you that I served with your son and it was he and I that conducted that rescue mission together to save some of our men. I wanted to tell you that I have never all these years forgotten Herb and the sacrifice he made for us."* I asked him for his address so I could write a lengthy letter explaining who I was and how important Herb's memory was to heal me and be a part of my ministry to Veterans. In my letter to Mr. and Mrs. Klug, I told them that I really wanted to visit Herb's graveside and if it was too painful for them to meet me, I would understand. They wrote back immediately and reassured me that when I came to Dayton, they would be there to pick me up at the airport, take me into their home, and take me to the cemetery to see Herb's grave. I had told them in the letter that I had become a Catholic Priest since the war. I did not want to shock them since they were of a different faith group than me.

I made the decision to go visit the Klug Family on a long weekend in July of 1991. They met me at the airport and took me into their home. They made me feel so comfortable even though I was frightened and anxious about being in the home of the parents of my dead buddy from Vietnam. The next day was Saturday and the plan was to go to visit the graveside of my buddy Herb. I had planned to tell the story of how Herb got killed at the graveside with his parents there. Ray, the father, told me that Beulah was sick and would not be joining us to go to the cemetery. I was frustrated because things were not going as planned. We stopped at a florist on the way to the cemetery to pick up a single, long-stemmed red rose to leave at the grave. We got to the graveside and I wanted to be alone for a while, but Mr. Klug stayed very close to me. I knelt down and laid the rose across the headstone. I felt awkward about speaking to Herb out loud with Ray standing so close to me—but when I saw he was not going to distance himself, I decided to just speak out loud anyway. I said to Herb, *Hi, Herb. I finally made it here. I am sorry it has taken 21 years to get here, but I want you to know that I have never once forgotten what you did in Vietnam on March 1. You died that others might live. I have been to see your name on the Vietnam Veteran Memorial. The work I do for veterans is done in your name and memory. We do this work together as I always feel your spirit with me. I will be back to see you and it won't take another 21 years to return."* When I finished, I got up and turned to Ray and saw him sobbing. I went to him and placed my arm around his shoulder and told him I was sorry that what I had said to Herb upset him so much. He replied that he heard everything I said to Herb and became so sad that those were feelings that he was never able to express to his son while he was living. He regretted never telling his son he loved him. When he was killed, he always felt that he had to be strong for Beulah and not break down nor show emotion towards her. We stayed in that hot afternoon sun for an hour, but it seemed like only a few minutes.

We went home and I was determined that after supper, I would tell the story of how Herb was killed with both of them together. The parents had a right to know. The Department of defense never goes into detail about the events surrounding the death of a loved one. It is basically a form letter of notification and condolence. As we sat around the kitchen table after supper, I began to tell the whole story, not leaving out any detail. One thing I confessed to was this. I told them how I have always felt guilty for Herb's death because it was my idea to go on this rescue mission that eventually took his life. If I had not initiated this action, he would not have volunteered to come with me and he would probably have finished his tour of duty and returned home. Immediately after I confessed this to the parents, Beulah grabbed my hand and squeezed it tightly and said firmly and without hesitation that they never blamed me nor anyone else for Herb's death. She said there was no need for confession because I had done nothing wrong. What happened, happened and it was just meant to be—that's all as she reassured me and gave me a big hug. She said we lost our only son but today we have a new son, and you will always be a part of our family. I felt such a release from years of guilt and doubt. It was as if a 100-pound weight had been removed from my shoulders. After, I asked them what happened when the body was shipped home. She began to describe the funeral services. She described how Herb was laid out in the casket with a glass cover placed over the top half of his body. That was done for fear that Beulah in her anguish would attempt to pick up his body to embrace it. They did not want that to happen because Herb's arm had been dismembered on the battlefield and so they had it lying by his side in the casket and, therefore, did not want the mother to disturb the body. When the Baptist Minister of their church came around to offer his condolences, he said to Beulah, *"You know Beulah, if you had been going to church more frequently, maybe God would not have taken your son."* I was so shocked to hear that a minister of God could be so insensitive to say such a horrible thing. I felt the rage well up inside me. I was in their home sitting there as a Catholic Priest—I wanted to crawl under the table. I then asked her what she did or said after that. Beulah replied angrily to the minister, *"Preacher, you are here to do a job. I expect you to go about your business and do it."* She never again set foot in a church. (**NOTE:** It was common in the 1970's to learn that many priests and ministers had taken a strong position against the war and often preached with hostility the sentiment of the anti-war movement. The sad part about all of this was that the warriors and family members of soldiers were trashed right alongside with the war. No distinction was made between the war and the warriors. It should have been: *hate the war but love the warrior!*)

I left the Klugs the next day to return home with a whole new family that I had adopted. I felt a tremendous healing and I believe God had offered a deep healing in the lives of my new family.

1991—1992 Drowning in Self-Pity

Over the years it became obvious to everyone, my friends, family and fellow priests that my drinking was getting out of hand. I enjoyed my cocktails and beer perhaps a little too much, but I was certain that I was not an alcoholic—after all, I never missed a day of work because of drinking, nor did I ever take a drink before 5:00 in the afternoon—the cocktail hour. On Thanksgiving night in 1991, I was involved in an automobile accident. No one was hurt but the car was a total loss. I was driving under the influence of alcohol. I realized that moment. He embraced me as if to say, *"Oh, thank God, you have come to realize what we have been so concerned about you for so long."* I entered into a residential treatment program for three months in the Guest House in Lake Orion, Michigan. This is a special program for Catholic Priests designed specially to meet their unique needs. This was a gift from God for me. I never thought I could live the rest of my life without another drink. I graduated from the program on Ash Wednesday, March 1, 1992. I have been in recovery ever since. I have enjoyed sobriety for seven years and I am grateful to God for giving me a second chance in life.

1995—The Great Jubilee Reunion

March 1st, 1995 marked the 25th anniversary of that fierce battle that took the lives of Herbert Wheeler Klug and 1LT Terrence Bowell and wounded 18 of our men. I called Ray and Beulah that morning to see how they were doing and I told them that I was remembering them on the 25th anniversary of the death of their son. They were so appreciative that I remembered. I still felt there was something missing in my healing story. I came up with an idea of a way to honor the memory of Herb and 1LT Bowell and also to give Ray and Beulah a very special gift. When I called Ray and Beulah that March 1st, I told her that I would like to give them a special gift that year to honor them and their son. I asked her what she thought of the idea of me trying to find as many of the members of the platoon for a reunion in Dayton to be held sometime later in the year. I told her that if I could pull this off, my plans would involve a Memorial Service at Herb's graveside and another one at the Dayton Vietnam Veteran Memorial where the names of all those killed in Vietnam from that city have their names inscribed. I asked her if would she be willing to open her home for a cookout afterwards so we could unwind and relax with each other. She graciously accepted. The difficult part of the task for me remained. How and where would I find the members of my lost platoon after twenty-five years. I had never maintained contact with any of them since the war. These men were scattered all over the United States. I began by digging through all of my military papers from 1969-1970. Among those papers, I found copies of orders for assignments and awards that would list many of my buddies' names and social security numbers since many awards were issued in large groups. With the first three digits of their social security numbers, I could determine what state they were from. I believed that most people never moved very far away from their home of record. I then purchased the National Telephone Book on CD-ROM and began my search. From those lists, I must have written 150 letters to people who I believed might have been members of my lost platoon. This whole process took about six months. In the letter, I introduced myself and asked whether they were the person I was looking for. I told them what I wanted to do—that is, schedule a reunion in Dayton in September of 1995 at a designated hotel to honor our two dead buddies from the platoon and to honor Herb's parents. I was never able to find the next of kin for Lieutenant Bowell who was from Littleton, Colorado, but we decided we would honor his memory as well. I eventually received 19 positive responses from the men I had served with. Of the nineteen people, fourteen agreed to come to the reunion and ten of them would bring their spouses. There was one particular letter I received from one of my buddies. I remembered him very well—Nick Aragon. He was a Mexican-American from New Mexico. We were very close buddies in Vietnam. The letter was particularly poignant. He wrote back telling me that he would definitely come to the reunion because he was one of those men who had been cut off from us on that fateful day. To learn that one of the reunion guys was one of those I helped rescue was overwhelming for me. It was a wonderful experience.

September came and one by one the members of the lost platoon began coming together for this reunion weekend. It was really awkward at first because, what do you say to someone whom you have not seen in twenty years after you have talked about the weather and each other's family? The ice-breaker was the photo albums. When everyone opened up their photo albums—then everyone began to relax and talk about old times—good and bad from the Vietnam War. We put pieces of the puzzle together and yet there were many, many missing pieces that we continue to find today in an attempt to complete the picture of what happened and how it impacted our lives. Ray and Beulah came to the hotel that evening to meet the men that served with their son. It was emotional and exciting at the same time.

The next morning, we got ready to go to the cemetery with Ray and Beulah leading the way. We gathered around Herb's grave and conducted a solemn Memorial Service remembering also our Lieutenant Terrence Bowell. We laid two wreaths there, one for Herb and one for Bowell. I led the service and asked James Edwards to preach. James Edwards was the Lieutenant who came to our platoon to replace LT Bowell. Edwards, after the war, also went to seminary and was ordained a Baptist Minister. We had an honor guard at the service with a twenty-one-gun salute and two buglers playing TAPS. When we finished that service, we proceeded to go to the Dayton Vietnam Veteran Memorial and conducted another powerful and emotional service there. I addressed the group at the service, reading the account of March 1st and the citation that Herb's family had received when they awarded him the second highest medal of valor, the Distinguished Service Cross. At the end of that service, I asked whether anyone wanted to share a few thoughts. Nick came forward and presented a red rose to Beulah and said to her in front of all of us, *"I want to thank you for my life. I want to thank you for the gift of your son, Herb. Had it not been for him and Phil, I would not be here standing in front of you. I am here today because of what Herb and Phil did and for that I will always be grateful."* Then he gave me and Ray and Beulah a big hug. Then Beulah came out and turned to the people with abundant tears flowing down her cheeks and she said to everyone, *I want to thank all of you folks for coming all the way to Dayton to be with us on this day. This is the nicest thing anyone has ever done for us in all these years."* It was comforting for them to know that many people remembered their son besides their immediate family.

Then we went to the home of Ray and Beulah for a cookout. We needed this outlet to unwind as the day was so emotionally charged. The healing that took place had been carried one big giant step forward from anything that had happened up to that point. We began to say our good-byes. It was painful, since we had just re-found each other after all these years. We made a commitment that we would continue to hold reunions every other year in a different part of the country. We held our last reunion in 1997 in Washington, DC, and went to visit the Vietnam Veteran Memorial together as a group to look up the names of Herbert Klug and Terrence Bowell, whose names happened to be placed one over the other.

1999—Alpha 6 Emerges from the Shadows

In addition to our biennial reunions of the Second Platoon for the last five years, I have attended the larger 199th Light Infantry Brigade reunion. They have designated me as their Chaplain. At these reunions, I seldom met anyone I actually served with except for about four or five veterans who served in the Third Platoon of Alpha Company. For the last few years, we have tried to locate other members of Alpha Company. Over a year ago, we located the whereabouts of our Company Commander,

Roland Merson. The Company Commander's cosign was "6"—hence Alpha 6. He had always refused to come to the reunions. This year, we were able to talk him into coming to the reunion in Washington, DC over the Memorial Day weekend. He arrived Friday evening from his home in West Virginia. I recognized him right away. He had not changed all that much. I recognized his gait and his stature. Alpha 6 and I joined the members of the Third Platoon at a restaurant and began to talk, to reminisce. The thing I remembered of him was that he was a fantastic Company Commander who always cared for his soldiers and protected us as best he could. He commanded our Company for nine months when the normal rotation for officers was six months. They made him rotate out in February of 1970. The Battalion Commander replaced him with someone that Merson was vehemently against. He advised him not to place this particular Captain in a command position. The Battalion Commander went against his advice and appointed him anyway. That is why on March 1st we ended up in the situation we did. The new Company Commander ordered us to walk down the same trail that we had come up on the previous afternoon, and the rest of the story is as I have illustrated at the beginning of this paper. This was why Alpha 6 had such a strong resistance to attending the reunions, or to have anything to do with the military after his career in the Army ended. He always blamed himself for what happened to us on March 1st. He kept saying to himself that he should have been there, that it should never have happened. He carried that awful burden of guilt for thirty years. It was so heart wrenching to hear him say that. I put my hand on his shoulder and told him that it was not his fault. It was the fault of the Battalion Commander and the new Company Commander. I assured him that we never, never blamed him for what happened to us. We loved him. He was the best. It was simply his time to leave. He began to relax at that point and he stayed talking to us until midnight. It was evident that deep healing was taking place. He had permitted himself to become vulnerable in opening his heart to let go of a poison he had been carrying for so many years, and replace it with the love of his men, the men who served proudly under his command.

I asked Alpha 6, Roland, to seriously consider coming to the Second Platoon reunion this August 6-9 in Southern California because that is the platoon that was hit bad on March 1st, and he really needs to see us just as much as we need to see him. The healing and reconciliation of past hurts continue with every new event and person that enters into our lives.

Summary – Conclusion

This story is entitled –**Journey from Darkness to Light-Spirituality as a Vehicle for Healing**, and is an ongoing saga. It is always a work in progress. As long as I live and breathe, the healing journey will always be a dynamic reality, and not a static one. The moment we stop moving in the direction toward light and healing, the moment we cease to take risks and become vulnerable, that is the moment we die. In the book of Deuteronomy, the sacred writer urges us to **CHOOSE LIFE**, and not death, choose life over death. Healing work is not easy. It is difficult and takes a lifetime to accomplish. It forces us to look squarely in the mirror and be afraid at what we see. We need to become friends with our pain, suffering, trauma and losses as well as with the blessings, the gifts and the uniqueness that we really are.

I use my story to help others develop their own unique and beautiful story. I give you my story that is the most precious gift I can give you, in the hope that you will one day give me your story. Remember that you are pure gift and the story you give me or to others is a rare and priceless work of art. Everyone's story is uniquely their own, just as there are no two people alike, there are no two stories alike. Once we embrace that reality, we will begin to experience holistic healing of mind, body and spirit. We will begin to enjoy inner peace and harmony throughout every part of our being.

Philip Salois Vietnam Veterans of America, National Chaplain

Appendix H
Dubrovnik: Conclusions of the First International
Conference

**Dubrovnik: Conclusions of the First International Conference
on the Psycho-Social Consequences of War**
April 26-April 30, 1998

1. The First International Conference on the Psycho-Social consequenc-
    es of War brought together 350 participants of the five continents.
    The multi-disciplinary orientation of the participants and their geo-
    graphic span enabled an exchange of views to be held between scien-
    tists and clinicians, decision-makers and war veterans and victims of
    war. This constituted its unique and innovative character.

2. The Conference made it possible to confirm that there is basis of
    post-traumatic stress disorders (PTSD) common to war veterans and
    victims of all armed conflicts and similar situations, regardless of their
    nature and geographic location. The Conference notes that, despite
    existing knowledge and the results of research in this field, many of
    those suffering from PTSD still do not benefit from the treatment
    based on that knowledge, or receive the financial compensation to
    which they should be entitled.

3. The Conference pointed out that there are other traumas as well,
    especially in the psycho-social sphere, which may vary in particular
    according to the nature of the conflict, the socio-political structure
    of the country and the attitude of their communities to war veterans
    and victims of war on their return home. These psycho-social conse-
    quences require further research as to their etiology and treatment.

4. The Conference considered the serious traumas suffered by women
    during armed conflicts or in similar situations and in particular the
    consequences of sexual violence, and the response to them. It noted
    that the efforts made in connection should be strengthened consid-
    erably and that research should be pursued.

5. The Conference also studied the problem of children and adoles-
    cents who were the witnesses or victims of violence during armed

conflicts and considered transgenerational problems. It believed that special attention should be paid to adolescents with a view to determining the intensity and gravity of any possible traumas so as to be able to treat them or prevent them from occurring, while stressing the serious consequences that the absence of such measures could have on society when such adolescents became adults.

6. The Conference also considered the special situation of those who had taken part in the UN Peace-Keeping operations and the traumas they may have suffered.

7. The Conference discussed the positive effects on the evolution of PTSD and the psycho-social consequences of war, of bringing the alleged perpetrators of war crimes, genocide or crimes against humanity before the International Criminal Tribunals of The Hague and Arusha and the considerable negative effects of the impunity of the perpetrators of such crimes.

8. The Conference highlighted the action to be taken by war veterans and victims of war, in particular within the WVF, to overcome antagonism between former enemies and the psycho-social consequences of war, and to contribute to peace.

9. The presentations made at the Conference and the discussions that followed therefore led to the following general conclusion:

9.1 The psycho-social consequences of war call for research and treatment which are of importance not only for the victim but also for the future of his or her community.

9.2 Such research requires a multi-disciplinary approach.

9.3 To pursue its action for this purpose, an Advisory Board to the WVF has been set up to determine the follow-up to be given to the Conference and to prepare the second International Conference on these subjects.

World Veterans Federation, 17 rue Nicolo, 75116 Paris, France

Appendix I
World Veterans Federation Wellbeing Statement

World Veterans Federation
Veterans Wellbeing Statement

We, the World Veterans Federation (WVF), observe that globally and despite good intentions, many veterans' needs are unmet. In recent times the focus has been on health issues, but the time is right to see that health is a part of wellbeing. We believe in the need for a holistic approach to veteran care.

As things currently stand, in some cases, these veterans are invisible and consequently unsupported; in others their plight is evident but unaddressed. As an organization with veterans' aid at its heart, we therefore call on all Governments and ex-service support agencies to work towards delivering universal wellbeing for former servicemen and women who were willing to put their lives at risk for their country.

This support must extend to their families; it is about more than just health and should encompass every aspect of their lives.

We ask that Governments and other responsible agencies open a dialogue with veterans, to discuss their real needs rather than simply telling them what is available.

We believe that only by asking veterans what they need will the tools to transform their lives be identified, and suggest that the garnering of real, quantitative evidence on a significant scale should be the norm in each country.

However, extrapolation of data alone is not going to promote universal veteran wellbeing. We expect more than *ad hoc* interventions or acknowledgment of service at public events. We advocate commitment to embracing all veterans, not just as wounded warriors, but as individuals deserving of dignity, provided with every opportunity to thrive and achieve their full potential.

We expect Governments, ex-service agencies and the world of business to deliver veteran support in the broadest sense, not just for the obvious few, but in a way that is conducive to promoting a rewarding life for all veterans and their families. Improving the lives of veterans is everyone's business, with prioritization of urgent, targeted help for the poorest and most vulnerable.

We believe that sustainable outcomes, based on demonstrably needed interventions and poverty reduction, are the keys to achieving universal wellbeing for veterans.

This is a project for the world. We believe that every veteran, without distinction of any kind, has the right to enjoy the highest attainable standard of physical and mental health and wellbeing that can be provided.

Our definition of wellbeing is "A state in which veterans and their families are best equipped to cope with adversity-however it presents itself." It is a comprehensive, veteran-centered approach based on the needs of the individual.

We acknowledge that geographic, socio-economic, cultural and other differences will mean that wellbeing translates uniquely in every country. Furthermore, we recognize the primary role and responsibility of Governments to determine their own path towards achieving universal veteran wellbeing, in accordance with national contexts and priorities.

We affirm the need for national ownership of health and wellbeing for all veterans aimed at eradicating discrimination toward them, promoting quality education, achieving gender equality, women's empowerment, providing decent work opportunities for economic self-sustainment, reducing inequalities and ensuring that action is taken to provide universal wellbeing for veterans throughout their life.

Political leadership and commitment are key to the success of this aim. Veterans are part of society, not apart from it, and investment in their wellbeing benefits the community as a whole.

We are defined by the way we treat the most vulnerable members of society and united by our common humanity. There must be a special emphasis on poor, vulnerable and marginalized veterans by recognizing that support systems must be strong, resilient, well-governed, accountable, integrated, veteran-centric and capable of providing quality support. Anything less in inadequate.

This statement formalizes the WVF's commitment to promoting and championing the cause of veteran wellbeing. It is a "living" statement which is designed to change as new issues inevitably become apparent.

It is our intention to move forward to promote universal wellbeing for veterans and, by consulting them directly, and in due course to create a world veteran human and social capital index for veteran care which charts progress. This in turn will promote exchange of knowledge and sharing of best practice.

Head of WVF Health and Welfare Division, Dr. Hugh Milroy

Appendix J
Excerpt of the Congressional Record Containing Fr. Phil's Opening Prayer Before U.S. House of Representative Session on February 27, 2019

The Office of the Chaplain
United States House of Representatives

Reverend Philip G. Salois

National Chaplain, American Legion

North Smithfield, RI

SPONSOR: Rep. David Cicilline, (D-RI)

Date of Prayer: 02/27/2019

One Minute Speech Given in Recognition of the Guest Chaplain:

Mr. CICILLINE. Madam Speaker, I rise today to recognize Father Philip Salois, who delivered today's opening prayer.

Father Phil is a native of Woonsocket, Rhode Island, and now lives in North Smithfield, Rhode Island, a community that I am proud to represent today in Congress.

He served our country in uniform during the Vietnam war as a combat Infantryman and earned the Silver Star for his valor.

After his service to our country, Father Phil felt called to service in another capacity. He was ordained into the priesthood on June 10, 1984.

A few years later, Father Phil joined the Veterans Administration in Boston, where he served as chief of the chaplain service from 1993 to 2015.

Today, he continues to minister to veterans in Rhode Island and all across America. We owe all of our service members and their families an incredible debt of gratitude.

The men and women of the United States Armed Forces represent our country's most important value of service, honor, courage, and sacrifice. This is especially true of Father Phil, who represents the very best of our country and my home State of Rhode Island.

I thank him for his service to our country and for being here today to offer the beautiful opening prayer. We are truly honored by his presence.

Opening Prayer Given by the Guest Chaplain:

Dear Lord, we beseech You to pour forth Your grace and blessings on all who gather to do the work that the people of America elected them to do.

We pray for peace and harmony when we disagree. We pray for the strength and will to work out our differences and to come up with the best solutions that will benefit society as a whole.

Watch over and protect the men and women in uniform, and safeguard them from all harm. And we pray You to bring them home safely to their families and friends.

We especially remember those who are held prisoner in foreign lands, those missing in action, as we continue to seek them out and bring them home to their loved one.

We make this prayer in Your name. Amen.

Appendix K
Complete List of Alpha Company Reunions

Complete list of Always Alpha Reunions
Provided by Fr. Philip Salois

1)   1995 - Dayton, Ohio with the first 15 or so members
2)   1997 - Washington, DC
3)   1999 - San Juan Capistrano, California
4)   2000 - Dayton, Ohio with the entire Alpha Company
5)   2002 - Littleton (Denver), Colorado for the Bowell family
6)   2004 - Boston, Massachusetts - where I hosted
7)   2006 - Portland, Oregon
8)   2008 - Tampa, Florida
9)   2010 - Saint Louis, Missouri
10) 2012 - Durango, Colorado
11) 2014 - San Diego, California
12) 2016 - Philadelphia, Pennsylvania
13) 2018 - Saint Paul/Minneapolis, Minnesota
14) 2020 - Branson, Missouri*
15) 2021 - San Antonio, Texas
16) 2022 - Nashville, Tennessee
17) 2023 - Rapid City, South Dakota

*After the 2020 reunion in Branson, Missouri, the group decided, since they were getting older with several members already having passed, that they should start meeting annually. Since that date the Always Alpha Reunions have been held each year.

Appendix L
2014 Joint Rhode Island House and Senate Resolution of Congratulations

2014-S2050

STATE OF RHODE ISLAND
IN GENERAL ASSEMBLY
JANUARY SESSION, A.D. 2014

SENATE RESOLUTION
CONGRATULATING FATHER PHILIP G. SALOIS FOR RECEIVING THE VETERAN OF THE YEAR AWARD FOR 2014 FROM THE UNITED VETERANS' COUNCIL OF WOONSOCKET

Introduced By: Senators Cote, Picard, and P Fogarty
Date Introduced: January 21, 2014
Referred To: Placed on the Senate Calendar

WHEREAS, Father Philip G. Salois currently serves as Chief Chaplain for the Veterans' Administration Boston Healthcare System, Chaplain for the VA New England Healthcare System, and President of the Lincoln Vietnam Veterans' Post 818. Father Salois was honored by the United Veterans' Council of Woonsocket for his lifelong work in helping Vietnam veterans and their families to overcome the trauma that results from combat and loss of life; and

WHEREAS, Before becoming a Priest, Father Salois served in Vietnam with the 199th Light Infantry Brigade. Armed only with a grenade launcher, he and a buddy braved the front and enemy fire to rescue comrades, despite the grave danger they faced. "Bringing bodies home, alive or not, was the objective." In the midst of all this chaos, confusion, violence and death, Philip G. Salois made a promise to himself that if he returned home without injury, he would acknowledge his destiny to God, and spend the rest of his life serving God, the Church and humanity; and

WHEREAS, Five years later, Salois answered the calling. After receiving the Silver Star for combat duty and his military service, Salois left the

United States Army to join the Catholic Ministry at La Salette in North Attleboro, Massachusetts; and

WHEREAS, Father Salois has over 44 years of exposure to combat stress, beginning with his own six-year experience in Vietnam, and through his service from 1984 to the present-day as a Priest helping those, like himself, who faced combat. Father Salois has also been a board-certified expert in traumatic stress since 2001, and is fluent in French and semi-fluent in Spanish and

WHEREAS, Father Salois has served as National Chaplain to the Vietnam Veterans of America organization since 1994, and as Massachusetts Department Chaplain to the American Legion since 1993. Other organizations for which Father Salois is a well-known supporter include AMVETS, Catholic War Veterans, Disabled American Veterans, Knights of Columbus, Military Chaplains Association, national Association of Veterans' Affairs Chaplains, National Conference of Veterans' Affairs Catholic Chaplains, and the Reserve Officers Association and

WHEREAS, In addition to receiving the prestigious Silver Star, Father Salois has received numerous other military awards including the Meritorious Service Medal, the Combat Infantryman's Badge, the Vietnam Service Medal, the Republic of Vietnam Campaign medal, the Air Medal, the Army Commendation Medal with three Oak Leaf Clusters, the Army Achievement Medal with two Oak Leaf Clusters, the Good Conduct Medal, the National Defense Service Medal, and the DAV Distinguished VA Employee of the Year Award; and

WHEREAS, Father Salois has also received numerous clergy awards including being the National Recipient of the Celtic Cross Award from the Catholic Veterans of America, the Life Achievement Award for Outstanding Service to the Veteran Community from Vietnamese-American Veterans of New England and Canada, the Veterans' Affairs Chaplain of the Year Award from the Military Chaplains Associations, the Chapel of Four Chaplains Humanitarian Award, the Chaplain of Four Chaplains Bronze Medallion Award, and the Knights of Columbus Lantern Award; now, therefore be it

RESOLVED, That this Senate of the State of Rhode Island and Providence Plantations hereby congratulates Father Philip G. Salois for receiving the Veteran of the Year Award for 2014 from the United

Veterans' Council of Woonsocket; and be it further

RESOLVED, That the Secretary of State be and hereby is authorized and directed to transmit a duly certified copy of this resolution to Father Philip G. Salois.

(Note: On March 20, 2014 an identical resolution was submitted by the House of Representatives)

Bibliography

Interviews:
1. Fr. Philip Salois, Interviewed by the authors – Julien Ayotte and Paul Caranci, Friday, April 28, 2023.
2. Fr. Philip Salois, Interviewed by the authors – Julien Ayotte and Paul Caranci, Friday, May 26, 2023.
3. Fr. Philip Salois, Interviewed by the authors – Julien Ayotte and Paul Caranci, Friday, June 16, 2023.
4. Fr. Philip Salois, Interviewed by the authors – Julien Ayotte and Paul Caranci, Friday, August 11, 2023.

Books:
1. Ayotte, Julien, Flower of Heaven, KDP Publishing, January 1, 2012.
2. Bellerose, Robert R., Images of America – Woonsocket, Arcadia Publishing, Dover, NH. 1997.
3. Cutter, Alan, Hope and Healing for Veterans: Resources for the Spiritual Journey, 2015. 2nd Edition edited by Ann Cutter. 2017.
4. Glasser, Ronald J., MD. 365 Days (50th Anniversary Edition with foreword by LT. General H.R. McMaster). New York. 1971.
5. Pickering, Alton Thomas, MD., Old Woonsocket - erastus & doc, Mowbray Company, Providence, RI. 1973.
6. Report of the National Conference of Vietnam Veteran Ministers, Tbilisi I International Conference of Veterans and Victims of War, Peaceful Caucuses – Peaceful World, Tbilisi. July 1999.

Periodicals:
1. American Legion Newsletter, A Lifetime of Healing, February 23, 2017 and February 28, 2017. Author anonymous. https://www.legion.org/magazine/236274/lifetime-healing.
2. Boston Globe, The, Hélène H Salois Obituary, March 23-24, 2013.
3. Burger, John, The Catholic Report, The Longest Battle. May 6, 2014.
4. Currey, Richard, Alive Day for Fr. Phil Salois, M.S., LaSalette The Americas. March 2022. Republished from The VVA Veteran Online, May/June 2014.
5. Feng, Patrick, The 199th Infantry Brigade. National Museum of the United States Army. https://armyhistory.org/the-199th-infantry-brigade/.
6. Howard, Henry, A Lifetime of Healing, American Legion. February 23, 2017. https://www.legion.org/magazine/236274/lifetime-healing.
7. Lennon, Frank, (Guest Columnist) The Providence Journal, Promises Kept. April 17, 2023, Page A1.
8. Lennon, Frank, (Guest Columnist) The Dark Side of America's Welcome Home: Vietnam Vets Recount Harassment and Disrespect. February 20, 2023. https://www.providencejournal.com/story/news/local/2023/02/20/vietnam-veterans-faced-scorn-and-rejection-when-returning-home-to-ri/69914945007/.
9. Milford Daily News, Combat Stress Unit Treats Soldiers for Psychological Wounds. August 19, 2005.
10. O'Brien, Nancy Frazier, Vietnam Memorial Veterans Find Healing, La

Salette Missionaries Newsletter, 2022. https://www.lasalette.org/reflections/faith/1127-vietnam-memorial-helps-veterans-find-healing.html.

11. Rhode Island Historic Preservation Commission, Statewide Historic Preservation Report for Woonsocket, Rhode Island. September 1976.

12. Stoffer, Jeff, In Remembrance of Fallen Friends and Comrades, American Legion Magazine. August 25, 2019.

13. Valley Breeze, The, Fr. Salois – 2014 Veteran of the Year.

14. Vietnam Veterans Memorial, The, The Wall-USA, Terrance Lee Bowell. http://www.thewall-usa.com/info.asp?recid-4956.

15. Wall of Faces, The, Herbert Wheeler Klug, Honored on Panel 13W, Line 71 of the Wall.

16. Woonsocket Centennial Committee, Woonsocket, Rhode Island - A Centennial History 1888 - 1988 Woonsocket Centennial Committee. 1988.

Internet Sources:

1. American-French Genealogical Society, Fr. Philip Salois, Class of 2014. https://afgs.org/site/fr-philip-salois/.

2. My Life, Salois, Philip, 74. https://www.mylife.com/philip-salois/e739429275306.

3. The Founding of Woonsocket and Brief Introduction (1888)
Woonsocket's Mill Rise of the 20th century
Reasons for the influx of French Canadians in the 1880's and 1890's
https://prezi.com/y3z76obtv5yi/woonsocket-interactive-history-the-rise-and-fall-of-lafayette-worsted-mill-and-itu-labor-union/

4. The Hall of Valor Project, Philip Gaston Salois, Los Angeles, CA. Silver Star.

5. Statement of Father Philip G. Salois, M.S., VISN 1 Chaplain Program Manager and Chief, Chaplain Service – VA, Boston Healthcare System, Before the Subcommittee on Health, Committee on Veterans' Affairs, March 11, 2004. https://corpora.tika.apache.org/base/docs/govdocs1/473/473996.pdf.

6. Veterans Advantage, Hero Vet Father Phil Salois Priest with a Silver Star Ministers to Those Who Have Seen the Blood, April 11, 2002. https://www.veteransadvantage.com/blog/veterans-advantage-awards/herovet-father-phil-salois-priest-silver-star-ministers-those-who.

7. Wikipedia, 199th Infantry Brigade (United States), https://en.wikipedia.org/wiki/199th_Infantry_Brigade_(United_States).

8. Wikipedia, Fort Ord, https://en.wikipedia.org/wiki/Fort_Ord.

9. Wikipedia, Lafayette Worsted Company Administrative Headquarters Historic District, https://en.wikipedia.org/wiki/Lafayette_Worsted_Company_Administrative_Headquarters_Historic_District.

10. Wikipedia, Langres, https://simple.wikipedia.org/wiki/Langres

11. Woonsocket-My Home Town on the Web; Woonsocket's Original Mill Villages. http://www.woonsocket.org/village.htm#:~:text=By%20the%201930%27s%2C%20the%20mill%20was%20being%20operated,The%20building%20was%20de-stroyed%20by%20fire%20in%201956.

Videos and Podcasts:

1. ChurchPop, Ryan, George, The Invisible Battlefield: How Military Chaplains are Fighting the Spiritual War. July 16, 2023.

2. The West Point Center for Oral History, One Chaplain's Story, Great Projects Films. https://westpointcoh.org/interviews/one-chaplain-s-story.

3. Thrall, Chris, T-Shirt Podcast, My Vietnam HELL, Father Phil Salois Silver Star, https://www.facebook.com/philip.salois. https://www.youtube.com/watch?v=njByz-eZM758. https://vva.org/chaplains-corner/. https://www.va.gov/.
4. Valley Breeze, The, On-line version, Nadeau, Salois recognized by Veterans' Council. December 11, 2013
5. Vietnam: The Battles, The Courage. A detailed look at the Longest Military Conflict in U.S. History! Three-disc set.
6. Vietnam Veterans Association, Vietnam War Veterans, Then and Now, Conversation with Father Philip Salois. Podcast, length = 55:55. https://www.vvthenandnow.com/father-philip-salois.

Press Releases:

1. Office of the Chaplain, The, Reverend Philip G. Salois, National Chaplain, American Legions, North Smithfield, RI. – Rep. David Cicilline (D-RI) One Minute Speech Given in Recognition of the Guest Chaplain. February 27, 2019. https://chaplain.house.gov/chaplaincy/display_gc.html?id=2869.

Photo Credits:

Photos from Fr. Phil Salois' personal collection.

https://images.search.yahoo.com/yhs/search?p=photos+of+fort+ord+-from+1969-1970&fr=yhs-tro-freshy&type=Y219_F163_204671_102220&hspart=tro&hsimp=yhs-freshy&imgurl=https%3A%2F%2Fi.pinimg.com%2Foriginals%2F2c%2F20%2F5d%2F2c205d1358c98c43a002bf76234656b5.jpg#id=77&i-url=https%3A%2F%2Fusarmykasern.files.wordpress.com%2F2021%2F12%2F135594214_999049390500781_6531467295471372604_n.jpg%3Fw%3D750&action=click.

About Julien Ayotte

Julien Ayotte graduated from Mt. St. Charles Academy (1959), received a B.S. degree (1963) and an M.B.A. (1969) from the University of Rhode Island, a Harvard Business School Management Development Program (1978) and a PhD (1992) from Columbia Pacific University.

Julien served as a high school business teacher, an Assistant Corporate Treasurer and Assistant Corporate Controller at Textron Inc., and as the executive director for two law firms, Partridge, Snow & Hahn and Mirick O'Connell. During this fourteen-year period at law firms, Ayotte was also an adjunct professor of finance and investments in the MBA programs at five universities in Rhode Island and Massachusetts.

He co-authored a financial planning book with Dr. Gerhard Harms, entitled *Wealth Building for Professionals* in 2001. His first two novels, *Flower of Heaven (2012)* and the sequel, *Dangerous Bloodlines (2014),* each received four national book awards. After *A Life Before* (2016), *Disappearance* (2017) was the 2018 Dorry Award Winner for Best Fiction and a 2019 finalist in the American Fiction Awards., *Code Name Lily (2018)* was a finalist in the 2019 Next Generation Indie Book Awards, and *Diamond and Pearls (2020)* was a finalist in the 2020 Top Shelf Awards. *The Treasure,* was released in late 2020, and *Spitting Images: A Harry Esten Mystery* in 2022.

Julien is a 2016 inductee into the Mt. St. Charles Academy Athletic Hall of Fame. He serves as a Trustee, Extra Ordinary Minister, Chair of the Parish Finance Council, and an altar server at his church.

He resides in Lincoln, RI with his wife Pauline. They are the parents of three grown children.

Also by Julien Ayotte

Flower of Heaven

Dangerous Bloodlines

A Life Before

Disappearance

Code Name Lily

Diamond and Pearls

The Treasure

Spitting Images: A Harry Esten Mystery

About Paul F. Caranci

Paul F. Caranci is a public speaker and the author of fifteen books. He served in several elected & appointed positions including as RI Deputy Secretary of State for eight years and the town council where he served for almost seventeen years. He has a BA in political science from Providence College and is a historian serving as a director on many history boards & commissions.

In 2015, Paul was awarded the Margaret Chase Smith American Democracy Award for Political Courage, the highest honor awarded by the National Association of Secretaries of State, for his role in exposing political corruption in his hometown of North Providence. His undercover work with the FBI, in breaking up what a federal judge called a criminal empire, is the subject of Paul's seventh book, *Wired: A Shocking True Story of Political Corruption and the FBI Informant Who Risked Everything to Expose It.*

Five of Paul's books were awarded special recognition. *The Hanging & Redemption of John Gordon: The True Story of Rhode Island's Last Execution* was voted one of the top five non-fiction books of 2013 by the Providence Journal. *Scoundrels: Defining Corruption Through Tales of Political Intrigue in Rhode Island* was the winner of the 2016 Dorry Award as the non-fiction book of the year. *The Promise of Fatima: One Hundred Years of History, Mystery and Faith; I Am The Immaculate Conception: The Story of Bernadette of Lourdes; and, Ear Candy: The Inside Story of Foxes & Fossils, America's #1 Cover Band,* were all named finalists in the International Book Awards in 2018, 2019 and 2023 respectively.

The movie rights to four of Paul's books were sold to a Hollywood production company and may one day be featured on the big screen.

Paul and his wife Margie have two adult children and four grandchildren.

Also by Paul F. Caranci

North Providence: A History & the People Who Shaped It

The Hanging & Redemption of John Gordon: The True Story of Rhode Island's Last Execution

Award Winning Real Estate Sales in a Declining or Depressed Market: Strategies for Thriving, Not Just Surviving, During the Bad Times

The Essential Guide to Running for Local Office: How to Plan, Organize and

Win Your Next Election

Monumental Providence: Legends of History in Sculpture, Statuary, Monuments and Memorials

Scoundrels: Defining Corruption Through Tales of Political Intrigue in Rhode Island

Wired: A Shocking True Story of Political Corruption and the FBI Informant Who Risked Everything to Expose It

The Promise of Fatima: One Hundred Years of History, Mystery and Faith

I Am The Immaculate Conception: The Story of Bernadette of Lourdes

Heavenly Portrait: The Miraculous Image of Our Lady of Guadalupe

Terror in Wichita: A True Story of One Woman's Courage and Her Will to Live

Before the End of the Age: Signs of the Coming Chastisement

Darkness at Dachau: The True Story of Father Jean Bernard

Ear Candy: The Inside Story of Foxes & Fossils, America's #1 Cover Band

Made in the USA
Middletown, DE
31 October 2023

41663374R00116